THIS  OR THAT? 4

or

EVEN MORE WACKY CHOICES
TO REVEAL THE
HIDDEN YOU

MICHELLE HARRIS AND JULIE BEER

NATIONAL
GEOGRAPHIC
KiDS

WASHINGTON, D.C.

The National Geographic Society is one of the world's largest nonprofit scientific and educational organizations. Founded in 1888 to "increase and diffuse geographic knowledge," the Society's mission is to inspire people to care about the planet. It reaches more than 400 million people worldwide each month through its official journal, *National Geographic*, and other magazines; National Geographic Channel; television documentaries; music; radio; films; books; DVDs; maps; exhibitions; live events; school publishing programs; interactive media; and merchandise. National Geographic has funded more than 10,000 scientific research, conservation, and exploration projects and supports an education program promoting geographic literacy.

For more information, please visit nationalgeographic.com, call 1-800-NGS LINE (647-5463), or write to the following address:
National Geographic Society
1145 17th Street N.W.
Washington, DC 20036-4688 U.S.A.

Visit us online at nationalgeographic.com/books

For librarians and teachers: ngchildrensbooks.org

More for kids from National Geographic:
kids.nationalgeographic.com

For information about special discounts for bulk purchases, please contact National Geographic Books Special Sales: ngspecsales@ngs.org

For rights or permissions inquiries, please contact National Geographic Books Subsidiary Rights:
ngbookrights@ngs.org

Paperback edition ISBN: 978-1-4263-2345-4
Reinforced library edition ISBN: 978-1-4263-2346-1

Printed in Hong Kong
15/THK/1

TABLE OF CONTENTS

Introduction 6

Super Smackdown 8

Odd Jobs 28

Outta This World 46

Delicious or Disgusting? 64

Hit the Road 82

Don't Miss a Beat 100

Mobile Madness 118

Get Festive 136

Pick Your Brain 154

Credits 174

GET PICKY!

CHOOSE **THIS:**
> Parachute to Earth from space.

CHOOSE **THAT:**
> Spend a year in space.

CHOOSE **THIS:**
> You have springs on your feet.

CHOOSE **THAT:**
> You rarely touch the ground.

CHOOSE **THIS:**
> Ice music

CHOOSE **THAT:**
> Volcano songs

DECISIONS! DECISIONS!

Every minute of every day we make choices about how we spend our time, what we like, and how we interact with one another. Most are minor, but when you add them all up, your decisions reveal what makes you YOU! THIS or THAT? WHICH WILL IT BE?

WELCOME TO THE BOOK OF CHOICES. Want to find out what superpowers would suit you? Or maybe you'd like to know what places you'd enjoy on a trip or what festivals you'd like the most? Each chapter offers you a series of options—some a little crazy, some serious, some downright silly, and some a little gross. Consider your choices with your friends—or even a parent—before you make up your mind. Then turn the page to see where your decision leads.

DECISION
DISSECTION!

KEEP COUNT
OF EACH TIME YOU CHOOSE

THIS!
or THAT!

AT THE END OF EACH CHAPTER, you'll get some professional help from Dr. Matt Bellace. He's a **stand-up comic**, a **motivational speaker,** and a **psychologist.** Dr. Bellace will analyze your choices and determine what your decisions say about you. Through exploration and analysis of the inner workings of your mind, he'll peel back your layers one by one and you won't even realize it!

Don't worry about making a wrong choice—there are none. If you've ever been called picky, get ready for loads of fun!

IN *THIS OR THAT?* 4, BEING PICKY IS A GOOD THING!

CHAPTER 1

SUPER SMACKDOWN!

When superheroes do battle, they are rarely on a level playing field. Whether it's wits versus brawn or technique versus finesse, each superhero puts forward his or her best asset to come out on top. In this chapter, you'll choose the superpower that's the best match for you.

CHOOSE
THIS:

You are **small** but **strong**, like **Ant-Man.**

or

CHOOSE
THAT:

You're **tough** on the outside but **sensitive** on the inside, like the **Thing.**

MUSE BEFORE YOU CHOOSE Big biceps. Thick skin.

If you CHOSE ⬇THIS:

Never underestimate the strength of an insect! Like ANT-MAN, who can shrink in size while increasing in strength, the RHINOCEROS BEETLE packs a punch. Growing up to six inches (15 cm) long, the beetle gets its name from the rhino-like horn on the male's head, but it also matches its namesake in brawn. It is able to lift 850 TIMES its own body weight—that would be the same as a human lifting NINE ELEPHANTS! That power comes in handy for the rhinoceros beetle when it has to escape predators. The beetle uses its horn as a shovel to quickly dig a hole in the dirt or to lift up DEBRIS from the forest floor and then hide underneath it.

Choice Nugget

Besides digging, the rhinoceros beetle uses its horn to fight off other males from encroaching on its feeding site. The size of the horn can be up to two-thirds of the beetle's body length.

If you CHOSE ⬇THAT:

COSMIC RADIATION is what gave the Thing—of the Fantastic Four—his rocky exterior and super strength. The MATA MATA TURTLE doesn't use its spiky shell and armored snakelike head to fight evil, but rather to blend in. The mata mata is camouflaged by leaves at the bottom of the shallow waters of SOUTH AMERICA, where it ambushes fish and invertebrates that pass by with its long, bumpy neck and vacuum-like mouth. But don't let the mata mata's tough side scare you—this turtle isn't dangerous to humans. In fact, it is quite sensitive to water quality and is easily harmed by pollutants.

CHOOSE THIS:

You can hit your mark like Hawkeye.

or

CHOOSE THAT:

MUSE BEFORE YOU CHOOSE

Wait and see. Sticky situation.

You can cast a wide net like Spider-Man.

If you CHOSE THIS:

Ready, aim, lunch! Like Hawkeye—of the Avengers—the **ARCHERFISH** has excellent reflexes. Instead of releasing an arrow, this fish fires a water cannon to capture its prey. With pinpoint accuracy, the archerfish shoots a stream of water from its mouth that can hit its target—such as an unsuspecting insect hanging out on a branch above the water—up to **FIVE FEET (1.5 M) AWAY**. Forming a tube with its tongue, it squeezes its **GILL** covers to fire a jet of water. Once the prey hits the water, the archerfish gobbles it up. And just because its weapon is water, it doesn't mean that it isn't forceful. Researchers say if an archerfish's water stream were to hit you, it would sting like a bug bite!

If you CHOSE THAT:

The song says Spider-Man can spin a web of any size, but can he spin one as long as two city buses? The Darwin's bark spider can! In Madagascar, **BARK SPIDERS** go to work spinning their webs across rivers and streams, attaching them to banks on either side. The largest web found was **82 FEET** (25 m) long. The one-inch (2.5-cm)-wide Darwin's bark spider spins silk that is among the **TOUGHEST** materials found in nature—even stronger than the material used to make bulletproof vests.

CHOOSE
THIS:
You can **run** at **supersonic** speeds like **Quicksilver.**

or

CHOOSE
THAT:
You could **beat** the **X-Men's Mystique** at **hide**-and-**seek.**

MUSE BEFORE YOU CHOOSE Good at tag. Spy for hire.

If you CHOSE
⬇THIS:

Don't be offended if someone tells you that you run like a mite. In fact, that's a mighty nice compliment! *PARATARSOTOMUS MACROPALPIS*, a type of mite that lives in Southern California, U.S.A., is the world's FASTEST land animal relative to its size. This sesame seed–size insect can sprint 322 body lengths per second. By comparison, the CHEETAH— which clocks the fastest actual speed of any land animal—moves at 16 body lengths per second. If you were able to run 322 body lengths per second like a mite, you could run 1,300 miles (2,000 km) in an hour!

If you CHOSE
⬇THAT:

How's this for an awesome party trick: You can shape-shift so no one can find you. The MIMIC OCTOPUS is an expert at it. Not only can it change colors, the mimic octopus can also impersonate a number of animals, scaring off potential predators.

It can flatten itself to look like a poisonous sole fish, swirl its arms to look like a lionfish, or change colors to look like a venomous sea snake. But it doesn't stop there—this octopus can even CHANGE its texture to match rocks, coral, and plants. Good luck spotting the mimic octopus the next time you go snorkeling!

CHOOSE THIS:

You have supersmarts.

or

ENGLISH
DEUTSCH
FRANÇAIS
ITALIANO
ESPAÑOL
PORTUGUÊS

CHOOSE THAT:

You can speak any language.

MUSE
BEFORE YOU
CHOOSE

A strong memory. Good at repeating things.

If you CHOSE ⬇THIS:

Imagine learning a kid's name at camp and then being asked what that kid's name was *20 YEARS LATER.* Think you'll remember? You'd have to have the memory of, well, a DOLPHIN! With some of the best memories in all of the animal kingdom, dolphins are able to remember other dolphins' whistles DECADES after they hear them. In fact, dolphins are considered to be one of the most intelligent species on Earth! They even use TOOLS; for instance, they carry sea sponges in their beaks to protect them from scrapes on rocks and urchins when checking out the ocean floor.

If you CHOSE THAT: ⬇

Watch what you say when you're around an African gray parrot. It might repeat what you have to say! GRAY PARROTS, one of the LARGEST parrots in Africa, don't have the ability to express original thoughts, but they can mimic what they hear. In the wild, they often mimic the calls of other birds. But in captivity, they are known to MIMIC the voices of the humans around them. But even though they can't carry an authentic conversation, they are fiercely intelligent. One African gray named Alex used English words to identify colors and shapes and was able to count up to SIX!

Think Twice!

Because they're mammals, dolphins have to come to the water's surface for air—about every seven minutes. When a dolphin sleeps, only half of its brain nods off; the other half remains awake to breathe and to keep an eye out for danger.

CHOOSE
THIS:
You have **springs** on your **feet.**

or

CHOOSE
THAT:
You rarely **touch** the **ground.**

MUSE BEFORE YOU CHOOSE

Famous footwear. No need for shoes.

Think Twice! Sloths are so slow-moving that algae actually grows on their fur, much like it does on trees, rocks, and other things that don't move! Algae gives sloths' fur a greenish tint, which helps them blend into the forest canopy.

If you CHOSE ⬇THIS:

MICHAEL JORDAN, considered one of the greatest basketball players in NBA history, was also one of the greatest dunkers. Jordan made sailing through the air from the free throw line and hanging on the rim a moment later look like child's play. In all, Jordan played **1,072 NBA GAMES** and scored **32,292 POINTS!** If you didn't get to watch him play before he retired, you might be able to find him on your shoes. The "Jumpman" logo, modeled after his famous dunk, is featured on the basketball shoes that bear his name.

If you CHOSE ⬇THAT:

THREE-TOED SLOTHS that live in the forests of Central and South America use those three long toes to grip branches, which allows them to spend just about all of their time aloft. But they don't move around much while they're in the trees. Sloths move at a rate of about 12 feet (3.7 m) per minute when they're on the go. The one time they do come down? For potty breaks—about once a week! Sloths **SLEEP** for up to **20 HOURS A DAY** and eat leaves and fruit that they find in trees. They get most of their water from the liquid in plants.

19

CHOOSE THIS:

You can **travel** to any time and any place **instantly.**

or

Choice Nugget

Originally introduced to Britain in the 1920s, police boxes were used by police officers to keep in touch with the police station.

POLICE

CHOOSE THAT:

You **see** the world in **slow motion.**

MUSE BEFORE YOU CHOOSE Trekking through the wilderness. Staring at flowers for *long* periods of time.

If you CHOSE
⬇THIS:

Step into the *Doctor Who* TARDIS, and you can rematerialize at another point in time on Earth or in another **GALAXY**. TARDIS, which stands for Time and Relative Dimension in Space, is the 1960s-looking London police box bioship that the Doctor uses to travel through time and over distances in the British TV show. Sure, this is all science fiction, but two physicists recently wrote a scientific paper explaining how a real TARDIS could, in theory, operate as a bubble of **SPACE-TIME**, moving backward and forward along a closed loop of time. The only problem: For the concept to work, it requires a certain exotic matter that so far hasn't been discovered. Alas, for now, you don't need to look out for flying police boxes.

If you CHOSE THAT: ⬇

Just think what your batting average would be if the ball were being pitched to you in slow motion. **SQUIRRELS** should really be recruited for the major league. To escape predators, squirrels—along with other small creatures—have evolved to see the world at a slower rate than humans do. That's because they are able to receive a lot of information in a short amount of time. Researchers measured how **FAST THE EYES** of small animals can **PROCESS** a blink of light. It turns out small animals process light so much faster than humans that, to them, life passes by in slower motion.

CHOOSE THIS:

You are a super smeller.

or

CHOOSE THAT:

You have ears on your feet.

MUSE BEFORE YOU CHOOSE

Follow your nose. Follow your ears.

If you CHOSE THIS:

Imagine being able to **SMELL** your dinner from a mile (1.6 km) away. Unfortunately, if your sniffer is that good, then you must be a turkey vulture. And if you're a **TURKEY VULTURE,** then your dinner wouldn't be pizza or a bowl of spaghetti; it may very well be roadkill. Turkey vultures have the best sense of smell of any bird. And they have a particular knack for sniffing out rotting flesh. You've probably seen turkey vultures circling low over open fields or hillsides, probably taking a whiff of a dead animal. Once a turkey vulture has found its meal, other scavengers, such as black vultures, eagles, and ravens, often join in on the feast. Yum!

If you CHOSE THAT:

ELEPHANTS may be Earth's **LARGEST** land animals, but they are quite sensitive. They're so sensitive, in fact, they can detect danger in their feet! Researchers found that when an elephant stomps its feet, it sends out a **SEISMIC WAVE** that can be detected by other elephants nearly 20 miles (32 km) away. This could be a way that elephants send and receive warnings that there's danger in the neighborhood. Those big elephant ears aren't for nothing, though. Elephants have good hearing, but their ears are also used to cool their bodies by radiating heat from blood vessels—plus, flapping their ears generates a nice cool breeze!

CHOOSE THIS:

You're **superfast, but** only in **short bursts.**

or

CHOOSE THAT:

You move **slow,** but you can go the **distance.**

MUSE BEFORE YOU CHOOSE Plenty of time to stop and smell the roses. Stuck to a tight schedule.

If you CHOSE ⬇THIS:

The **HAWK MOTH** doesn't even need a cape to be one of the fastest flying insects on the planet. This moth has been clocked at speeds over **33 MILES** an hour (53 km/h). With narrow wings and thick bodies, the hawk moth is an acrobatic insect—capable of hovering in one place just like a humming-bird. And like the hummingbird, they seek out **NECTAR**, using a superlong proboscis—over a foot (30 cm) long!—to snag pollen from flowers like orchids. Their superhero weakness? A short life span. They only live about a week as adults. Talk about short and sweet!

If you CHOSE THAT: ⬇

When you're a **GALÁPAGOS TURTLE**, your superpower isn't your speed. These giant reptiles—which can weigh as much as 500 pounds (227 kg)—chug along at a rate **17 TIMES SLOWER** than you cruise on your walk to school! Yep, there was a reason the hare mocked the tortoise. But where the Galápagos tortoise lacks in giddy-up, it makes up for in longevity. The oldest one on record was over **170 YEARS OLD!** Tortoises are among the longest-living animals on the planet—so there's plenty of time to forget any race they might have lost!

LET'S SEE WHAT **YOUR CHOICES** SAY **ABOUT YOU.**

DOC TALK ...

PSYCHOLOGIST
DR. MATT BELLACE
DISSECTS YOUR
DECISIONS ...

ANALYZE
THIS!

If you mostly picked **CHOOSE THIS,** you're a dynamic, intelligent person who enjoys a fast-paced life. You love the latest smartphone app or video game, and you just can't wait for the next one to come out! You're ahead of your time and for good reason; your brain's processing speed is faster than the average Joe. This is exciting for you but might leave others feeling left behind. As long as you're aware that the rest of us are not always as quick on the uptake, perhaps you can bring us up to speed!

ANALYZE
THAT!

If you mostly picked **CHOOSE THAT,** you're a quirky soul who enjoys being different. You've got tremendous talents, but you're not interested in doing things the way they've always been done. In fact, you might purposefully confuse people with your life decisions. You're like the professional athlete who also composes classical music, or the guy with a Ph.D. who does stand-up comedy. You're very in-tune with the world around you and you like getting a reaction from people. Your challenge is knowing when to take a breather and let someone else share the spotlight.

CHAPTER 2

ODD JOBS

Ready to think about the future? Your future job, specifically? There are countless things you can do as a career—from teaching to being an artist, scientist, or doctor. Then there are jobs you may have never even heard of. Did you know that there are scientists whose job it is to fly in airplanes into hurricanes? It's true! Some jobs are kind of dangerous—and other jobs are a little wacky. This chapter is about all kinds of odd jobs that you can choose. Some are even jobs animals do! Select the one that suits you and see what direction your career is headed!

CHOOSE **THIS:**

You **fly** a **plane.**

or

CHOOSE **THAT:**

You **ride** a **camel.**

MUSE BEFORE YOU CHOOSE   Fly solo. No need for water breaks.

If you CHOSE THIS: ⬇

Imagine you're a delivery driver, but instead of cruising city streets, your route is the skies of the **ALASKAN FRONTIER**. Bush pilots carry food, supplies, and mail to isolated areas all over Alaska, sometimes to villages that don't even have roads. They also provide medical evacuation. Alaska has twice the area of any other U.S. state, but it is the fourth least populated. That means the most efficient way to get around is often by small plane! Alaska can have severe weather, and flying through the mountainous terrain is technical. Being a bush pilot isn't easy, but someone has to do it!

If you CHOSE ⬇THAT:

Hold on, it may be a bumpy ride. But what better way to make sure the **PYRAMIDS** at **GIZA** are safe and secure than to patrol by camelback? Egyptian guards cruise the area around the **4,500-YEAR-OLD** pyramids on dromedaries, which are perhaps better suited for the desert environment than any motorized vehicle. Considered one of the seven ancient wonders of the world and now a **UNESCO WORLD HERITAGE** site, the three pyramids were built for three kings of the fourth dynasty. The largest, called the Great Pyramid, built for the King Khufu, was originally 481 feet (147 m)—that's more than one and a half times as tall as the Statue of Liberty.

CHOOSE

THIS:

Someone does your dirty work.

or

CHOOSE

THAT:

You clean up after others.

MUSE BEFORE YOU CHOOSE Plenty of snack breaks. An eye for detail.

If you CHOSE ⬇ THIS:

When you're a RHINO, it's nice to have a little help keeping those hard-to-reach areas clean. Thank goodness for OXPECKERS, eight-inch (20-cm)-long brown birds with striking yellow or red bills. These small African birds cling to the backs of rhinos and other big-game animals—such as elephants and hippos—and nibble ticks, flies, and maggots living there. It's a win-win situation: The annoying insects are kept in check for the rhino, and the oxpecker gets a delicious snack!

If you CHOSE THAT: ⬇

Good friends pick each other's nits. Now that would make a great T-shirt for a CHIMPANZEE. Chimps—the closest living relatives to humans—often GROOM one another, picking dirt, dead skin, fleas, ticks, and, yes, lice, out of each other's fur. Scientists say this is an important social interaction for chimps—it creates bonds between family members and keeps things friendly within the larger social community. It's also relaxing. Sometimes the chimp that is being groomed will doze off! Often after one chimp has been groomed, he or she returns the favor and picks through the other's fur. Grooming sometimes lasts for hours!

33

CHOOSE THIS:

Handle snakes.

CHOOSE THAT:

Handle fire.

Think Twice!

Snake handling is risky business! Milkers have years of experience handling venomous snakes. This isn't a job for rookies. Don't try this at home!

MUSE BEFORE YOU CHOOSE

Quick hands. In the hot seat.

If you CHOSE THIS:

Here's a job that you can really sink your teeth into, or rather, it can sink its teeth into you. **SNAKE MILKERS** handle deadly snakes in order to collect **VENOM** that can be used for scientific study. Here's how it works: Snake milkers carefully pick up a venomous snake—a rattlesnake, for example—and press on its head and neck to expose its **FANGS**. The fangs rest over a collection funnel, and a very small amount of venom is released and stored in a collection tube. The venom is freeze-dried into a powder and sent to scientists who turn it into antivenom—a medicine that helps people recover from snakebites. It is also studied to treat heart attacks, blood clots, and high blood pressure.

If you CHOSE THAT:

Be prepared to take some heat on this job. **HOTSHOTS** are elite wilderness firefighters who are trained to respond to fires in remote areas with very little support. There's no sleeping on this job: During wildfire season, Hotshots are on call 24 hours a day, 7 days a week. Because crews are often dropped off in remote areas to fight fires, they wear about **40 POUNDS** (18 kg) of gear—including chain saws and shovels—and they wear flame-resistant clothing. Hotshots dig trenches, called fire lines, to contain fires and clear away brush from encroaching fire.

CHOOSE **THIS:**

Study what is **overhead.**

or

CHOOSE **THAT:**

Examine what is **underfoot.**

MUSE BEFORE YOU CHOOSE

Turbulence ahead. Bring a flashlight.

If you CHOSE
↓THIS:

During a big STORM, your instincts probably tell you it's a good idea to hunker down inside and wait it out with a nice big cup of cocoa. But if you're a HURRICANE HUNTER, your job is to head into the storm aboard a special airplane that studies weather. Flight METEOROLOGISTS who work for the National Oceanic and Atmospheric Administration (NOAA) travel on turboprop aircraft that can withstand high winds, but the meteorologists have to have stomachs that can withstand some serious turbulence. While riding out the bumps, they gather scientific data to produce weather forecasts—such as temperature, wind speed, and wind direction. That information helps the rest of us on the ground know if the storm is headed our way, how big a storm we need to prepare for, and how quickly it might arrive.

If you CHOSE THAT:↓

If you're someone who likes to dig deeper into a subject and really unearth the facts, then SPELEOLOGY—the study of caves—may be the job for you. There are 17,000 CAVES in the United States alone. In fact, every state in the U.S. except Rhode Island and Louisiana has at least one cave in it. The largest and most common caves are formed by a chemical reaction between groundwater and limestone bedrock. Caves are like natural underground laboratories for scientists. Besides their spectacular geologic features—such as stalactites and stalagmites, minerals shaped by slow-dripping water—they are home to fascinating species, including the olm, a pale-pink blind amphibian, and worms that glow.

Choice Nugget

When hurricane hunters fly through the "eye" of a hurricane—the center of the storm—there is little wind, no precipitation, and sometimes even blue skies!

CHOOSE
THIS:
Go **fishing** in **rough seas.**

or

CHOOSE
THAT:
Go to work **under** the **sea.**

MUSE BEFORE YOU CHOOSE   Smells a little fishy. Feeling queasy. Good breath control.

If you CHOSE ↓THIS:

For the casual FISHERMAN, a day of baiting a hook and throwing out a line is the ultimate in relaxation. But if you're a crab fisherman in the Bering Sea, hauling in a catch is no picnic. It's so chilly that ice can form on the boat's deck. If that weren't dangerous enough, 700-POUND (318-kg) crab cages that you haul in can knock you overboard. And talk about seasickness alert: Waves toss boats and relentlessly splash the crew. Occasionally boats will even capsize. Fishermen wear "SURVIVAL SUITS"— waterproof suits that protect them from hypothermia if they get thrown into the sea. Why on earth would you want to be a crab fisherman? There is a payoff: the paycheck. Crab fishermen are well compensated for their hard, dangerous work.

If you CHOSE ↓THAT:

Imagine that your job's uniform is a wet suit, and you are fully equipped with scuba gear. Nope, you're not a scuba instructor or even a coral reef explorer—you're an underwater welder! That's right, UNDERWATER WELDERS dive with a torch and other welding gear, often inspecting and repairing equipment such as offshore oil platforms, pipelines, and ships. Underwater welders are trained in both welding and diving and can only work for a few hours before they need to surface and spend time in a DECOMPRESSION CHAMBER. The work is strenuous, but at least you don't have to worry about chatty co-workers!

CHOOSE THIS:

Make a meal fit for a queen.

or

CHOOSE THAT:

Prepare food at Earth's highest kitchen.

MUSE BEFORE YOU CHOOSE

Talk about royal pressure. The peak of your career.

40

If you CHOSE ↓THIS:

Can you pour a bowl of corn flakes? Make a jam sandwich? Prepare a pot of tea? Then you might want to apply to be Queen Elizabeth's ROYAL CHEF! The BRITISH MONARCH is known for her simple tastes. A typical lunch might be grilled fish on a bed of wilted spinach. A FAVORITE ASSORTMENT of tea sandwiches includes cucumber, smoked salmon, and honey mustard—with the crust cut off, of course. There is one thing the queen especially loves—chocolate! Chocolate mousse, chocolate pie, and chocolate biscuit cake (a chocolate cake with cookies inside) are among her favorites, according to her former personal chef.

If you CHOSE THAT: ↓

Like outdoor cooking? How about in the highest kitchen on Earth? That would be on MOUNT EVEREST, where Sherpas—an ethnic group who live in the Himalaya renowned for their climbing skills and endurance at high altitudes—are hired as mountain guides, porters, search-and-rescue workers, and cooks. Sherpa cooks prepare meals at Everest Base Camp, located at 17,590 FEET (5,361 m) above sea level, and at Camp 2, located at 21,000 feet (6,400 m), before climbers set off to ascend the world's highest mountain. And no, Sherpas don't serve up boring old trail food like peanuts and granola. They serve things like garlic soup, pasta, fried eggs, and veggies. Food is important on Everest: Extreme altitude is hard on the body, and you'll need your strength to make it to the summit.

Choice Nugget

New Zealander Sir Edmund Hillary and Sherpa Tenzing Norgay—the first mountaineers to summit Mount Everest—weren't fancy with their food. They fueled up on canned fish, chicken noodle soup, apricots, and tea.

41

CHOOSE THIS:

Garbage collector.

or

CHOOSE THAT:

MUSE BEFORE YOU CHOOSE

Heavy lifting. Work sure stinks. Don't leave fingerprints.

Window washer.

If you CHOSE THIS:

GARBAGE COLLECTING is true dirty work. In fact, it's considered to be one of the most dangerous jobs in the United States. Why? Well, for starters, workers are exposed to all the muck that people toss out—often things that they're not supposed to, like batteries that can **OOZE ACID**. Yuck! Garbage collectors can also get cut on broken glass or lightbulbs that poke through plastic bags. And then there are the live dangers—such as rats, raccoons, and sometimes even bears that hang around garbage looking for a quick and easy meal. Being a garbage collector requires **EXTREME CAUTION!**

Think Twice!

Dubai can get strong winds that swirl around the Burj Khalifa and send the window washers swaying—which is no fun when you're hanging from a building 160 stories in the air!

If you CHOSE THAT:

Best not look down. The **BURJ KHALIFA**, located in **DUBAI, UNITED ARAB EMIRATES**, is the world's tallest building, and it's covered in 24,000 panes of glass. About 60 workers are charged with keeping the outside of those windows clean. To do so, window washers repel down the **2,716-FOOT** (828-m)-tall building on ropes, wearing harnesses and helmets. Keep in mind, Dubai is in the desert and there's a lot of dust. It takes about three months to clean all of the windows, and once the crew is finished, they start all over again.

ANALYZE THIS!

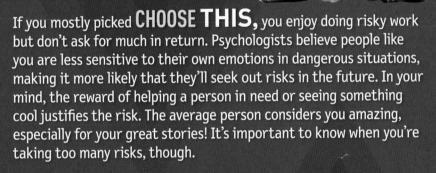

If you mostly picked **CHOOSE THIS,** you enjoy doing risky work but don't ask for much in return. Psychologists believe people like you are less sensitive to their own emotions in dangerous situations, making it more likely that they'll seek out risks in the future. In your mind, the reward of helping a person in need or seeing something cool justifies the risk. The average person considers you amazing, especially for your great stories! It's important to know when you're taking too many risks, though.

ANALYZE THAT!

If you mostly picked **CHOOSE THAT,** your personality favors being behind-the-scenes but still part of the excitement. You're a calculated risk-taker who values making it home in one piece. In addition, you take tremendous pleasure in helping others realize their dreams. You don't require much praise or attention, because lending a helping hand and being near the action is reward enough.

CHAPTER 3

OUTTA THIS WORLD

Pack your bags and brush up on your planets! In this chapter you'll have to decide between some pretty way-out choices where the sky's not the limit. Do you want to take a trip to the moon, or would you rather float around the International Space Station? Are you a big dreamer, or do you like to check the details? You'll find these answers and more in this chapter. So get ready for a far-out adventure—the universe is calling!

CHOOSE THIS:

Parachute to Earth from space.

or

CHOOSE THAT:

MUSE BEFORE YOU CHOOSE

Fear of heights.
Homesickness.
Zero gravity.

Spend months in space.

If you CHOSE THIS:

You'd feel quite a rush if you jumped from the edge of space back to Earth. Only three daredevils have ever accomplished such an extreme **SPACE DIVE**: Joe Kittinger in 1960, Felix Baumgartner in 2012, and Alan Eustace in 2014. Talk about an elite group! But jumping from the **STRATOSPHERE** isn't something you can just get up and decide to do. To get ready for their jumps, these adventurers underwent weeks and weeks of specialized training. Then they donned protective jumpsuits and dangled from helium-filled balloons, which lifted them up, up, and away. Once at the edge of space, at an altitude of about 25 miles (40 km), these thrill seekers took the plunge, free-falling back to Earth! After navigating the vast darkness of space, jumping from the high dive at the pool might not seem so tough.

Choice Nugget

Skylab missions racked up a total of 171 days and 13 hours in low-Earth orbit.

If you CHOSE THAT:

If you were an astronaut in the 1970s, you might have had a chance to be a human guinea pig on **NASA'S SKYLAB** mission. After the Apollo moon landings, the scientists at NASA started to think about ways to test how the human body would deal with longer-term space missions—important if humans were ever to live on Mars. So they built a floating space lab—Skylab. Three different astronaut crews took turns living on the orbiting station, for weeks at a time, undergoing rigorous medical checkups. The result? NASA found that humans could indeed live in what some people call **ZERO GRAVITY**, or more accurately, microgravity. And, as an added bonus, the astronauts were able to work for a long time without getting tired!

CHOOSE **THIS:**

You have your **head** in the **clouds.**

Choice Nugget

The Mars Climate Orbiter came within 37 miles (60 km) of the red planet.

or

CHOOSE **THAT:**

You **focus** on the **details.**

MUSE BEFORE YOU CHOOSE · Being called an "airhead." Fact-checker. Lost in thought.

If you CHOSE THIS: ⬇

If you're a big dreamer, SpaceX is the place for you. In the past, government scientists and agencies have done all the grunt work to get us Earthlings into space. But there's a new game in town—private companies such as SpaceX are helping to get payloads into space. It's not just government paper-pushers who get to dream about space exploration. SpaceX has been around since 2002, and in that short time, the company's accomplishments are nothing to sneeze at. It has designed rockets and invented a free-flying spacecraft called Dragon that has delivered supplies (and will soon deliver astronauts) to the International Space Station. Ready to relocate? SpaceX operates from a 4,000-acre (1,600-ha) facility in **MCGREGOR, TEXAS, U.S.A.**, and has more than 3,000 employees. See, a little space dreaming isn't so bad after all.

ELON MUSK, FOUNDER OF SPACEX AND TESLA

If you CHOSE THAT: ⬇

If math and science are your thing, NASA sure could have used your help back in 1999 during the **MARS CLIMATE ORBITER** program, a mission that was supposed to study Martian weather for a year. When engineers programmed the $125 million thrusters for the weather station that would orbit Mars, they calculated everything with pinpoint accuracy—or so they thought. As the craft reached Mars, instead of going into orbit, it burned up in the atmosphere! The mishap was pretty basic: One team of engineers used **ENGLISH UNITS** (such as inches, feet, and pounds) for measurements, and the other used metric—and that's not a good thing during a space mission whose success depends on the accuracy of even the tiniest details.

CHOOSE **THIS:**

You've lost your **sense** of **smell.**

or

CHOOSE **THAT:**

All you **smell** is **rotten eggs.**

MUSE BEFORE YOU CHOOSE No more body odor. Omelets will never look the same. Perfume is lost on you.

If you CHOSE ⬇ THIS:

You might think ASTRONAUTS would enjoy a rich, decadent chocolate cake to round out a mission in space, but the yumminess would actually be totally lost on them. Why? Because in space, astronauts lose their sense of smell. In other words, the cake would taste more like cardboard than cocoa. Most of our sense of taste is based on smell, and since hot air doesn't rise in a MICROGRAVITY ENVIRONMENT, scientists think that aromas don't float either. Serving food in pouches doesn't help either, since they limit the delicious smells that waft up to the nose. So while you might have amazing celestial views, space is not the place to indulge in a blowout foodie fest.

If you CHOSE ⬇ THAT:

Get ready to take your sniffer to the COMET 67P/C-G. Scientists think this smelly cosmic object was ejected from the KUIPER BELT, a region of space located just beyond Neptune's orbit. Comet 67P/C-G stinks like rotten eggs! When scientists from the European Space Agency (ESA) analyzed the comet's atmosphere, they found a foul-smelling mixture that included hydrogen sulfide, formaldehyde, and ammonia, which are all super-stinky substances. Why were the scientists sniffing around this comet anyway? The ESA's Rosetta mission visited this SHOOTING STAR to learn about what happens when an icy comet approaches the sun. Scientists believe what they find could give clues to how life may have started right here on Earth. Maybe a little stink is OK after all.

> ## Choice Nugget
>
> To overcome the boredom of bland foods, astronauts crave eats that are hot and spicy.

CHOOSE THIS:

You're **always** **dropping things.**

or

Choice Nugget

In 1965, astronaut Ed White dropped a white glove outside of the Gemini 4 spacecraft. It stayed in orbit for a month before burning up in Earth's atmosphere. His other glove was recently sold on eBay.

CHOOSE THAT:

You're **always** **leaving** things **behind.**

Bungling balls. Homework is often missing. Lots of trips to the lost and found.

If you CHOSE ⬇THIS:

The next time you FUMBLE a ball, don't be too hard on yourself. Even highly trained spacewalkers have been known to have butterfingers from time to time. But when you drop things in space, it's a lot harder to get them back. A $100,000 TOOL BAG, a spatula, a bolt, and a washer have all gone bye-bye. The tool bag was lost when an astronaut tried to clean up a leaking grease gun, and the bag, which wasn't secured, drifted away. But the bosses at NASA'S MISSION CONTROL don't yell and scream when this happens. They understand how hard it is to work in microgravity while wearing bulky gloves and a spacesuit that makes you look like the Stay Puft Marshmallow Man!

If you CHOSE THAT:⬇

If you tend to leave things behind, then you'll feel right at home in space. Why? Lots and lots of objects get left in orbit, from old SATELLITES and abandoned rockets to many smaller things, such as nuts and bolts. In fact, there are thousands and thousands of pieces of space junk whizzing around the Earth right now, and you won't find orbiting garbage trucks cleaning it up. Plus, this stuff isn't gently FLOATING around up there, it's zooming around at 17,000 miles an hour (27,400 km/h)! With all that clutter, sometimes accidents do happen. For example, in 2009 a Russian satellite crashed into and destroyed an American one, and this created a huge cloud of debris and more space junk. Maybe leaving things behind, in space at least, isn't the BRIGHTEST IDEA.

CHOOSE

THIS:

You like to **stay connected.**

or

CHOOSE

THAT:

You're **happy** to **let things go.**

MUSE
BEFORE YOU
CHOOSE

Separation anxiety. Umbilical cords. No looking back.

If you CHOSE ⬇THIS:

Pack your bags for a heart-thumping space walk on the INTERNATIONAL SPACE STATION! Sure, the only thing keeping you from floating off into deep space is a tether that serves the same purpose as a leash that keeps your dog from bolting down the street. Tethers allow astronauts to spend five to eight hours working outside the space station, giving them the security to repair equipment or perform experiments without having to worry about floating away. And just in case a spacewalker does get disconnected, the astronauts carry a rescue aid that works like a jet pack and helps them fly back to safety.

Choice Nugget

In 2012, two 17-year-old Canadians launched a Lego man on a helium balloon that made it to 85,000 feet (25,000 m). That's more than double the typical cruising altitude of a commercial airplane!

If you CHOSE ⬇THAT:

Chickens in space?! No, we're not talking about Gonzo in some Muppets movie. We're talking about a rubber chicken known as CAMILLA CORONA, the space chicken. Camilla is no stranger to spaceflight. She has traveled to the upper levels of our atmosphere in a hot-air balloon five times. That's one high-flying bird! She also helps with science experiments. In March 2012, Camilla measured high-energy solar protons (the charged particles that create the aurora borealis) when a solar storm was in full swing. Camilla measured the protons from point-blank range at 120,000 FEET (36,576 m). Now that's something to squawk about!

CHOOSE
THIS:

You prefer to be in the shadows.

or

MUSE BEFORE YOU CHOOSE

Under the radar. Privacy. Popularity. Autographs.

CHOOSE
THAT:

You crave the spotlight.

Choice Nugget

NASA's Jet Propulsion Laboratory is located across from some of the rocket boys' original test sites.

If you CHOSE THIS:

If you were one of the original "ROCKET BOYS," people weren't going to be paying a lot of attention to you. But experiments by these "boys" were super important. You see, before astronauts could take to the sky, scientists had to invent the means to get them there. And in the fall of 1936, a few enterprising young scientists did just that. They tried to send rockets into the sky, but unlike today, there weren't news crews following their every step, and no one was posting about it on social media. In fact, people at the time thought they were a little bit spacey! So the group went to a canyon in the Arroyo Seco, just outside of Pasadena, California, U.S.A., to TEST THEIR ROCKETS. After some early mishaps, including an oxygen line that caught fire and sent flames shooting into the sky, the rocketeers succeeded. Their research laid the groundwork for all American rockets to follow, even though the spotlight missed them at the time!

If you CHOSE THAT:

In 2012, more than three million people glued their eyes to their computer screens to watch the much anticipated Mars landing of the CURIOSITY ROVER. Since the landing was streamed live, if anything had gone wrong, everyone would have known about it immediately. Talk about pressure! You can bet the NASA scientists at Mission Control had sweaty palms. Plus, the mission was no walk in the park. First, a parachute slowed the rover when it was about seven miles (11 km) above Mars; then eight small rockets guided the craft until a sky crane could lower it to the ground. The rover, about the size of a MINI Cooper, descended for more than seven minutes. Then it successfully landed in GALE CRATER—and immediately became an Internet sensation!

CHOOSE

THIS:

Throw a curveball extra far.

or

CHOOSE

THAT:

Lift 600 pounds.
(273 kg)

MUSE BEFORE YOU CHOOSE Lightning-fast speed. Pumping iron. Megamuscles.

If you CHOSE ⬇THIS:

Grab your glove and get ready to play a pickup baseball game on the moon. Imagine the views of Earth! But that's not the best part. On the moon you can throw a ball SIX TIMES farther than you can on Earth. Prefer golf? You can hit a golf ball six times farther on the moon. And dunking a basketball would be a breeze because you would be able to jump six times higher. How is all of this possible? The MOON only has 17 percent of the gravity that keeps us Earthlings grounded. That makes things super easy. So get ready to show off your super skills, but don't forget that once you came back down to Earth, you'll be back to normal again.

If you CHOSE ⬇THAT:

Choice Nugget

In February 1971, astronaut Alan Shepard hit two golf balls on the moon during the Apollo 14 mission.

On the INTERNATIONAL SPACE STATION, moving objects that weigh hundreds of pounds takes just a gentle push. Astronauts living in an environment where they experience the force of gravity only one-millionth as strong as it is on Earth find that lifting weights is child's play. SO WHAT'S THE DOWNSIDE? Without resistance from GRAVITY, astronauts have a hard time keeping their muscles in shape. They lose muscle mass and bone density, which can turn these superfit athletes into weaklings with chicken arms! To keep in shape, astronauts use an exercise machine nicknamed "the Beast." NASA has added cylinders of air to this machine to provide the resistance that gives astronauts the workouts they crave. And what kinds of "beasts" are they? The max setting on this monster is the same as lifting 600 pounds (272 kg) on Earth. Talk about doing the heavy lifting!

ANALYZE THIS!

If you mostly picked **CHOOSE THIS,** you've got a sharp mind, you're even-keeled, and you're a thrill-seeker! That's a rare combination of attributes for one person. It's like being a really fast and strong athlete who also happens to be the smartest student in school. The phrase "one-in-a-million" applies to your personality, though it might be more like "one-in-ten-million." The good news is these abilities will serve you well anywhere you travel, including in outer space.

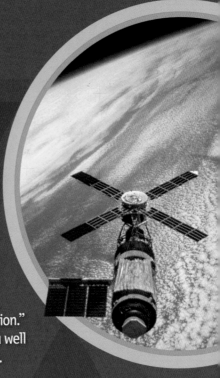

ANALYZE THAT!

If you mostly picked **CHOOSE THAT,** you're a detail-orientated person who is not afraid of hard work. You get excited by challenges that intimidate others, like doing extra-credit math assignments or solving a Rubik's Cube. You're not the most social person, but that really doesn't bother you. In your mind, life is easier when you're left alone to do your work, even if the work is programming your own fun video games. It's great that you thrive in social isolation, but remember that you need other people to be happy in the long term, so make sure to set aside some time to spend with friends!

CHAPTER 4

DELICIOUS or DISGUSTING?

Have you ever been told "Don't make a face before you taste this?" We often make our minds up about whether or not we're going to like a food before we've given it a fair chance. This chapter is all about making food choices. Just keep in mind, sometimes the item you order on a menu doesn't show up quite the way you were expecting it to. Bon appétit!

THIS:

Eat **fruity** ice cream.

or

THAT:

Eat **Eskimo** ice cream.

Choice Nugget

In Singapore, the aroma cast from durian is so despised that it is banned from trains! Many Southeast Asian hotels also ask guests not to bring the football-size fruit into their rooms because of the odor it leaves behind.

MUSE BEFORE YOU CHOOSE Not your typical sorbet. Interesting mix-ins.

If you CHOSE ⬇THIS:

Strawberry, mango, coconut—fruit flavors are pretty standard fare when it comes to ice cream. But order a **DURIAN** cone at the Chinatown Ice Cream Factory in New York City, and you're in for a real stinker! The ice cream is made with durian, a Southeast Asian fruit that is prickly on the outside with a custard-like consistency inside that's described by some as smelling like a dead animal! But some people love the taste and don't even pinch their noses when they order up a double scoop!

If you CHOSE ⬇THAT:

Don't expect to bite into a chocolate-covered ice-cream bar if you order an Eskimo ice cream in **ALASKA.** This treat, made by Alaska natives, is typically made from reindeer fat, seal oil, fresh berries, and sometimes ground fish. The concoction is whipped together so that the end product is light and airy. Also known as **AKUTAQ,** the delicacy is rich in protein and fat and is traditionally served during special occasions— after a boy's first hunt or at a funeral. And it's served in a bowl, not on a stick!

CHOOSE THIS:

Dive into mashed potatoes.

or

CHOOSE THAT:

Throw Food.

If you CHOSE THIS:

No need for a fork to enjoy these mashed potatoes! At **POTATO DAYS** in Barnesville, Minnesota, U.S.A., people of all ages wrestle in a ring marked off by hay bales and filled with mashed potatoes. Regular wrestling rules apply—the winner is the one who pins his or her opponent. Expect to be covered from head to toe in goopy spuds, but don't worry, there's a hose for cleaning up afterward. In an effort to not waste food, the **MASHED POTATOES** are made from dried spuds that have expired and aren't intended for consumption. So no nibbling in the middle of a headlock!

If you CHOSE THAT:

MOORES DORSET KNOB BISCUITS

Why throw away a perfectly good biscuit? There could be only one good reason: You're at a **"KNOB-THROWING"** competition in Dorset, England. (A knob is a round handmade biscuit.) The goal of the competition is to toss a knob as far as you can. But rules must be followed! You can only toss underhand, and one foot must remain on the ground for the toss to count. If a **BISCUIT BREAKS** upon landing, an umpire determines where the measurement should be taken. The person with the **FARTHEST TOSS** gets a plaque— and their biscuit, of course. All of the other biscuits are crushed and fed to local chickens.

CHOOSE

THIS:

Have
Frankenstein
over for **dinner**.

or

CHOOSE

THAT:

Bring Buddha
to your **table**.

MUSE
BEFORE YOU
CHOOSE

Monstrous appetite. Enlightened conversation.

If you CHOSE ⬇ THIS:

If you made this pumpkin your table centerpiece, you'd be sure to scare off your friends! "PUMPKINSTEINS" are made by a California, U.S.A., farmer who grows pumpkins—and watermelons!—to look like the creature in Mary Shelley's novel *FRANKENSTEIN.* The pumpkins are grown inside of a mold, and as they get bigger, they start to take a monstrous shape. It took four years and hundreds of thousands of dollars to get the pumpkins just right. Farmer Tony Dighera had to find a pumpkin variety that would grow big enough to fill the mold but would also be small enough to finish ripening. The spooky squash isn't cheap—each one costs about $100.

If you CHOSE ⬇ THAT:

Here's a fruit you might hesitate to sink your teeth into. PEARS SHAPED LIKE THE BUDDHA are grown on trees in China and shipped around the world. Using the same growing concept as that used for the Frankenstein pumpkins, a plastic mold is attached to a pear as it begins to grow on a tree, and as it gets larger it starts to look like the Buddha. The company that harvests these also grows baby-shaped pears. The pears are sold for around eight dollars, and the farmer who grows them says they represent GOOD LUCK.

CHOOSE **THIS:**

Eat a gummy bear.

or

CHOOSE **THAT:**

Munch on a chocolate bar.

MUSE BEFORE YOU CHOOSE Sticky fingers. S'more anyone?

If you CHOSE
↓THIS:

If you ate just one of these GUMMY BEARS your tummy would be aching! What's coined as the "world's largest gummy bear" weighs FIVE POUNDS (2.3 kg) and is roughly the size of a football. These giant gummy bears come in a variety of flavors—from lime to cherry to sour apple—and cost around ten dollars each. Are you more of a gummy worm person? Cue the toothbrush! The same company that makes the oversize bears makes the world's largest gummy worms, which are more than two feet (0.6 m) long!

If you CHOSE
↓THAT:

WILLY WONKA would even be impressed by this chocolate bar. Weighing in at 12,190 POUNDS (5,529 kg), a chocolate bar made by a Chicago candymaker was nearly 3 feet (0.9 m) high and 21 feet (6.4 m) long. That's the equivalent weight of 120,000 Hershey's chocolate bars. It was made using 5,500 pounds (2,495 kg) of SUGAR, 2,000 pounds (907 kg) of milk powder, 1,700 pounds (771 kg) of cocoa butter, and 1,400 pounds (635 kg) of chocolate liquor. The bar would be far too tempting for Augustus Gloop—the boy in *WILLY WONKA AND THE CHOCOLATE FACTORY* who fell into the chocolate river. Think you would take a nibble?

CHOOSE

THIS:

Eat pink snow.

or

CHOOSE

THAT:

Eat yellow snow.

Choice Nugget

Watermelon snow is nothing new. During Captain John Ross's 1818 expedition to search for the Northwest Passage, Ross reported finding fields of red snow. He didn't see it fall from the sky and thought it was the work of an iron-nickel meteorite. A compelling theory, but alas, he was wrong.

MUSE BEFORE YOU CHOOSE Smells sweet, but is it a stinker? They say looks are deceiving.

If you CHOSE THIS:⬇

Watermelon-flavored **SNOW** cones are delicious. Snow found in the great outdoors that looks like watermelon, not so much. Called "watermelon snow," "red snow," and even "snow blood," this naturally occurring phenomenon isn't the work of snow beasts, but rather algae that likes to grow in subzero temperatures. You may think of algae as being green, but one kind, *CHLAMYDOMONAS NIVALIS,* is reddish pink. When you take a whiff of watermelon snow, it even smells a little sweet. But however tasty it may look or smell, don't eat it. It's possible the **ALGAE** could be contaminated with bacteria and could make you sick. So no munching!

If you CHOSE ⬇THAT:

You'd eat yellow snow?! Well, who could blame you, especially when it's a tasty blend of mango, banana, and pineapple! A shave ice shop in California, U.S.A., has a **"SECRET MENU"** that features a flavor called Don't Eat Yellow Snow, which combines these tropical flavors. (Another flavor, I Dream of Monkey Brains, is made with strawberry and orange ice-cream flavors along with sweetened condensed milk.) People have been munching on flavored ice for centuries. Legend says that the **ROMAN EMPEROR NERO** sent his slaves to the snowy mountains to collect ice, and it was served to him topped with nectar, fruit pulp, and honey. Hmmm, those all sound suspiciously **YELLOW.** Maybe Nero ate yellow snow, too!

CHOOSE **THIS:**

Drink **filtered water** in space.

or

Think Twice!

Before you dismiss the idea of drinking recycled water in space, consider this: The water that astronauts drink is probably purer than the water you drink here on Earth!

CHOOSE **THAT:**

Drink **bottled water** from Loch Ness.

MUSE BEFORE YOU CHOOSE   Exactly how filtered is it? Mysterious flavor.

If you CHOSE ⬇THIS:

When you drink water aboard the International Space Station, you're an outstanding **RECYCLER!** That's because **93 PERCENT** of the liquids that are generated in space—from pee to sweat—are captured and turned into filtered drinking water! OK, before you get totally grossed out, check out how it's done: Body fluids and even water left over from, say, brushing your teeth, are collected in a distiller that spins to produce artificial gravity and move the wastewater. Contaminants go to the sides of the distiller's drum, and the steam that is left is collected, filtered, and turned into water. The cool thing about recycling water like this means that humans could, in theory, live for long periods of time away from Earth without needing new supplies of water.

If you CHOSE ⬇THAT:

You can take a swig of water collected right from the lake that thousands of people flock to every year to see if they can spot a famously elusive sea monster. A water bottling company sells bottled water from **LOCH NESS** to tourists who might want to take home a little bit of the **SCOTTISH WATERS** with them. Several sightings of an aquatic animal have been reported over the years, which some have said could be the sole survivor of the plesiosaurs, marine reptiles that lived during the Triassic period. Photos have been examined and reexamined; ships have cruised the water with high-tech sonar. There isn't any conclusive evidence that there is a "Nessie" in the waters, but folks still like to venture to the Scottish Highlands and have a look for themselves.

CHOOSE THIS:

Eat Ants.

GIANT
TOASTED
ANTS
Net Wt. 25g

- THE WORLD'S LARGEST ANT
- NUTTY BACON LIKE TASTE
- RARE DELICACY OF THE GUANE INDIANS

or

**MUSE
BEFORE YOU
CHOOSE**

If peanuts
had legs. A
beverage with
strong roots.

CHOOSE THAT:

Drink Weeds.

If you CHOSE THIS:

In Colombia, the ultimate snack treat may very well be roasted ants. That's right: ANTS! A type of leaf-cutter ant is harvested in the mountains of northern COLOMBIA. It's as big as a cockroach, and the females—which are the ones hunted for snacking—are captured when they are bloated with eggs. The eggs make them especially rich in protein. The ants are roasted in a pan and are said to have an earthy, nutty taste and the texture of stale popcorn. Think someone would have to pay you to eat a roasted ant? It's quite the opposite in Colombia. A pound of ants runs about $40, which means they aren't an everyday snack food.

If you CHOSE THAT:

In the UNITED KINGDOM, a popular soda flavor is dandelion and burdock. That's right, DANDELION— the yellow lawn weed that is also popular in salads (burdock is a type of root). Fruit juice is sometimes added to the beverage for a little sweetness. A soda with ingredients plucked right from the ground? Surely this must be a passing fad? Nope. Dandelion and burdock drinks have been around for generations. And it isn't the only beverage that has "roots" in a plant. ROOT BEER, though usually artificially flavored now, was originally made from a variety of roots and became the most popular soft drink in America during the 1800s!

LET'S SEE WHAT YOUR CHOICES SAY ABOUT YOU.

DOC TALK ...

PSYCHOLOGIST **DR. MATT BELLACE** DISSECTS YOUR **DECISIONS ...**

ANALYZE THIS!

If you mostly picked **CHOOSE THIS,** your personality is drawn to things that might gross most people out. You don't let fear take over but instead think more like a scientist when experiencing new things. This quality allows you to stay calm when others are panicking over a mouse running around, but might be dangerous when you're tasting poisonous food. You would make an excellent doctor, able to treat all the nasty things that grow on the body. To some people that kind of work sounds awful, but to you it probably sounds awesome.

ANALYZE THAT!

If you mostly picked **CHOOSE THAT,** you're a social person who is drawn to big events and tourist attractions. In fact, you find that having lots of people around makes it easier to step outside your comfort zone and try new things. The only downside of your style is that it relies heavily on other people. Choose your friends wisely, and remember that a little alone time can be nice too sometimes.

CHAPTER 5

HIT THE ROAD

Strap on your backpack and get ready for an adventure. In this chapter you'll discover everything from where movie stars like to hang out to where you can have a close encounter with a volcano. Or maybe you'd rather hang with fluffy fur balls in a cozy café or swing with monkeys in the rain forest. Choose carefully though, because everything may not be as it seems.

CHOOSE **THIS:**

You like bright lights.

or

Choice Nugget

Las Vegas is home to the world's largest neon sign, a 40-foot (12-m)-tall cowboy known as Vegas Vic.

CHOOSE **THAT:**

You like dark nights.

MUSE BEFORE YOU CHOOSE Sunglasses. No need for a night-light. Stargazing.

If you CHOSE THIS: ⬇

Pack your bags because you're heading to the brightest place on Earth—**LAS VEGAS, NEVADA, U.S.A.** This city is jam-packed with neon lights, and since there isn't an "off" switch, you can guarantee it never gets dark! More than **350 MILLION PEOPLE** visit this twinkling town every year. That's more than five times the population of France! Some of those visitors make it to the Neon Museum and its Boneyard, an outdoor exhibition space where you can see vintage neon signs undergoing restoration, along with those that still shine. But if you want to see the **BRIGHTEST LIGHT** of them all, head to the Luxor Hotel and Casino on the Las Vegas Strip. The Luxor's Sky Beam shines light ten miles (16 km) into space. With the lights on 24/7, there's one thing you don't want to forget to pack—your shades!

If you CHOSE THAT: ⬇

If you visit **CHILE'S ATACAMA DESERT,** you can leave your umbrella behind. The **ATACAMA** is known as the driest place on Earth, so you probably won't see any raindrops. But you will see plenty of stars. Pull on your fleece and head out into the night to see why this area really shines. It has some of the **DARKEST SKIES** on Earth. And since few people live in the Atacama's remote mountains, the sky is not only clear but also free of "light pollution" (artificial light—such as from streetlights and house lights). This arid region is home to cutting-edge scientific observatories and **TELESCOPES PEERING** out into the cosmos. In fact, it was from here that astronomers mapped the supermassive black hole at the center of the Milky Way galaxy. Now that's far-out!

85

CHOOSE

THIS:

Swim with bubble gum.

or

Think Twice!

A surge pool at the Pancake Rocks is known as the Devil's Cauldron because waves gush in during high tide and splash against the rocks, sending sprays of water higher and higher up the sides of the "cauldron."

CHOOSE

THAT:

Hike on top of pancakes.

MUSE
BEFORE YOU
CHOOSE

Keep an eye out for sharks. Sticky situation. Ocean spray.

If you CHOSE ↓THIS:

If you take this dip, you'll be heading out into cold ocean waters. *Brrrrr!* You'll soon see that the BUBBLE GUM IN THE OCEAN isn't for chewing, but rather it's a species of cold-water coral! Referred to as bubblegum coral (*Paragorgia arborea*), this type of coral has bundles of ORGANISMS (called polyps) on the ends of its branches that look just like gum balls. Each "gum ball" has eight tentacles that capture plankton and other small bits of food drifting in the ocean currents. While this coral grows in the cold waters of the north Pacific and north Atlantic Oceans, it's located deep down, at depths of 650 to 4,200 feet (200–1300 m).

If you CHOSE ↓THAT:

Save your maple syrup, these pancakes aren't what you had in mind! You're headed to PUNAKAIKI, NEW ZEALAND—on the west coast of the South Island—to see the country's famous PANCAKE ROCKS. These kind of "pancakes" started to form some 30 million years ago under the sea as marine creatures died and fell to the bottom of the ocean. Then, intense pressure from the water and depth turned the critters into solid rock. As the rocks rose above the surface, rain and wind shaped them to look like mom's homemade flapjacks. If you want to see the formations up close, be sure to pack a rain jacket. When ocean water enters caverns below the pancakes at high tide, PLUMES OF SPRAY SHOOT UPWARD between the stacks to douse visitors.

CHOOSE THIS:

Go to the movies.

or

CHOOSE THAT:

Go to the library.

MUSE BEFORE YOU CHOOSE Ghost stories. Peace and quiet. Buttery popcorn. No shouting.

If you CHOSE ⬇THIS:

Get your star power on! It would be pretty cool to watch a movie while sitting next to a famous **HOLLYWOOD STAR**, right? Well, you can at Cinespia, but the problem is those stars are, well, in the graves that are surrounding you at the Hollywood Forever Cemetery in Los Angeles, California. That's right, **CINESPIA** gives moviegoers the opportunity to watch films from picnic blankets right in the middle of a graveyard. Creepy! But don't get too nervous! There's more fun than fright at this fascinating cemetery, which first opened in 1899. It's the final resting place for hundreds of Hollywood's famous actors, producers, and directors. There's even a photo booth, so you can snap pics to document the occasion. Just don't be surprised if a ghost shows up in the shot!

If you CHOSE ⬇THAT:

This **LIBRARY** is one of the most famous in the world. And it's smack-dab in the middle of midtown Manhattan in **NEW YORK CITY!** The New York Public Library first opened its doors more than 100 years ago, and today it welcomes millions of visitors (and bookworms) every year. Pull up a chair and get to reading; or if people-watching is your thing, head over to the main reading room. It can hold as many as 1,000 people, which is quite a crowd! The library's collection contains some **15 MILLION ITEMS**, including baseball cards and comic books. With reading material in more than 1,200 languages and dialects, and current newspapers from all over the globe, nobody can ever say there's nothing to do in this *biblioteca* (that's library in Spanish, bub).

CHOOSE THIS:

You're a
cat person.

or

CHOOSE THAT:

You're a
dog person.

MUSE BEFORE YOU CHOOSE

Scratchy
tongues. Wet
licks. Cat hair.
Dog breath.

If you CHOSE THIS:

Get ready for a **PURR-FECT** adventure at one of Japan's cat cafés. These restaurants cater to people who love cats and also love to snack! Since cats aren't allowed in some **TOKYO** apartments, the cafés sprang up as places for cat lovers to unwind while surrounded by furry friends. Stressed-out office workers and tourists missing their fluff balls at home visit these snack shacks for a dose of feline fun. And if the cats are meowing after your food, you can buy them their own snacks, such as boiled chicken. Some bistros rescue stray cats, nurse them back to health, and then allow customers to adopt them. Don't worry, there are strict rules protecting the kitties from too much cuddling!

If you CHOSE THAT:

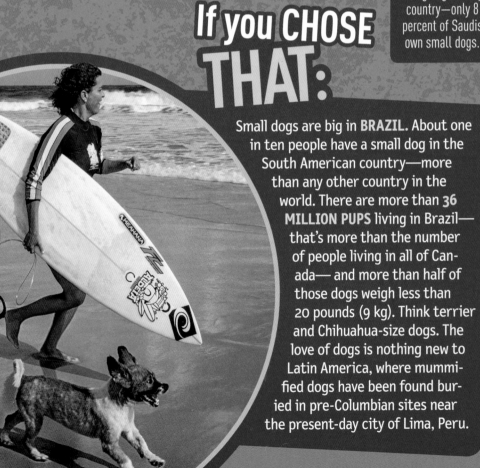

Small dogs are big in **BRAZIL.** About one in ten people have a small dog in the South American country—more than any other country in the world. There are more than **36 MILLION PUPS** living in Brazil— that's more than the number of people living in all of Canada— and more than half of those dogs weigh less than 20 pounds (9 kg). Think terrier and Chihuahua-size dogs. The love of dogs is nothing new to Latin America, where mummified dogs have been found buried in pre-Columbian sites near the present-day city of Lima, Peru.

CHOOSE **THIS:**

Mail a letter underwater.

or

CHOOSE **THAT:**

Mail a letter from the end of the Earth.

MUSE
BEFORE YOU
CHOOSE

Pack your swimsuit. Earmuffs required.

If you CHOSE ⬇THIS:

If you ever find yourself scuba diving off the coast of JAPAN, you're going to want to write home and tell your family about it— mostly so you can take advantage of an underwater mailbox that is situated at a depth of 33 feet (10 m). Divers who have bought a WATERPROOF postcard in the town of Susami and scribbled out their messages with an oil-based marker are the only ones who are able to use what is considered the world's deepest UNDERWATER mailbox. The red mailbox was installed 15 years ago to draw attention to the area when a fair was passing through. It worked: Tourists drop in some 1,500 pieces of mail every year!

If you CHOSE THAT: ⬇

Goudier Island, ANTARCTICA, is home to 2,000 gentoo PENGUINS ... and one post office. Why would a tiny, soccer field–size island in Antarctica have a post office? It actually processes 70,000 pieces of mail for more than 100 countries annually during its operating months of November to March, mostly from tourists on cruise ships that flock to the island twice daily. But don't expect the post office to send your mail express! It takes letters anywhere from two to six weeks to be delivered. Scientists on the island study the penguin population, and the black-and-white residents can be seen padding around the post office grounds.

Choice Nugget

As if getting a postcard from under the sea isn't fancy enough, you can also buy an edible postcard made from squid jerky to send to friends from the underwater mailbox!

CHOOSE

THIS:

Outrun lava.

or

CHOOSE

THAT:

Bathe among glaciers.

MUSE BEFORE YOU CHOOSE You can look, but you can't touch. Warm on the inside, chilly on the outside.

If you CHOSE ⬇THIS:

Hawaii's Big Island is, as you might imagine, the biggest of the HAWAIIAN ISLANDS—and it's still growing! Kilauea VOLCANO has been erupting since 1983 and creates enough lava every day to resurface a 20-mile (32-km) two-lane road! Most of that lava has gone straight to the ocean in LAVA TUBES, adding new layers to the island. Since it began erupting, 500 new acres (202 ha) have been added to the island's overall square footage! Recently, a new vent formed, and the lava is moving in a different direction. Locals are keeping a close eye on its progress, hoping it doesn't get too close to homes and businesses. But you can blink an eye and not miss too much when it comes to watching Kilauea's lava flow: It moves at a rate of about 15 to 30 feet (5 to 9 m) per hour.

If you CHOSE THAT:⬇

GLACIERS may dot the island country of ICELAND, but you can enjoy taking the plunge outside in a toasty swimming pool year-round! Thermal pools are heated naturally by underground volcanic activity. One of the most popular is Blue Lagoon, which is—you guessed it—a brilliant blue, thanks to the MINERALS inside it. People have been bathing in geothermal pools since the time of the Vikings—and a few of those pools still exist. Iceland's placement on the Mid-Atlantic Ridge makes it a super-active volcanic place, and Icelanders have used that to their advantage: Some 85 percent of the country's homes are heated by captured thermal energy.

CHOOSE THIS:

Watch the city go by below.

or

CHOOSE THAT:

Hear the sounds of the forest all around you.

MUSE BEFORE YOU CHOOSE

Cityscapes and urban views. Treetops and animal noises.

If you CHOSE THIS:

In about the amount of time that you can hold your breath, you can zip in an elevator to the observation deck of Taipei 101, one of the **TALLEST** buildings in the world. Located in Taiwan, **TAIPEI 101** is 1,670 feet (509 m) tall. Tourists can take a trip up to the observation deck and peek over the edge (behind a guard fence) to check out what's happening on the city streets 1,286 feet (392 m) below. But perhaps more impressive than its height is how fast you travel to the top floors. Pressurized elevators speed along at 38 miles an hour (61 km/h). The shape of the **SKYSCRAPER** resembles a pagoda, and its sectioned look is inspired by bamboo.

If you CHOSE THAT:

Until 20 years ago, the only people who cruised through **COSTA RICA'S** forest canopy were scientists who wanted to observe the jungle from a good vantage point—and who also needed a quick way to get from Point A to Point B. Today, tour groups offer rides on zip lines, where you can view the forest the same way a monkey does, from the top down. Observation towers can be more than **70 FEET** (21 m) high and nearly a half mile (0.8 km) apart, but don't worry: You're strapped in with a harness as you zip between platforms on wires at speeds of 50 miles an hour (80 km/h) or faster!

Choice Nugget

The number eight is considered lucky in Chinese culture, and the number holds special significance at Taipei 101: The building has eight upward flaring sections, and the whole building is supported by eight columns.

97

ANALYZE
THIS!

If you mostly picked **CHOOSE THIS,** you have a real sense of adventure, even if the journey makes you uncomfortable at times. You're a throwback to an earlier era when explorers weren't afraid to deal with unpleasant moments in order to reach their destination. You value the reward of an experience more than you worry about the possible consequences.

ANALYZE
THAT!

If you mostly picked **CHOOSE THAT,** you're a person who considers both the details and the big picture when making decisions. When it comes to adventure, you know that it's fun to do cool things, but it's even more fun when those things are happening in amazing places. You're what others call a visionary because you can step back and see the forest for the trees. Of course, this big-picture thinking does come at a price. It's very expensive and time-consuming to visit the hot spots, but I'm sure your high-functioning brain can handle preparing for your travels.

CHAPTER 6

DON'T MISS A BEAT

Do you march to the beat of your own drummer, or do you prefer to sing along with the crowd? Do you like your music deafening, or do you prefer to keep things chill? In this chapter you'll answer questions about a lot of different—and unexpected—kinds of music and musical instruments. From the crescendo of a school choir to the *plunk, plunk, plunk* of a banana keyboard, your choices will determine what you hear.

CHOOSE THIS:

Intense sounds.

CHOOSE THAT:

Mellow music.

MUSE
BEFORE YOU
CHOOSE

Adrenaline rush.
Soothing sounds.
Crowds.
Coziness.

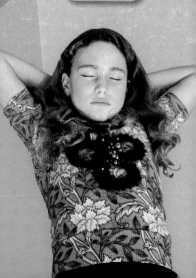

If you CHOSE THIS:

If you could have attended the 2010 FIFA WORLD CUP soccer tournament in South Africa, chances are your ears would have been buzzing the whole time. But this buzzing wouldn't have come from a swarm of bees overhead. Instead, it would have been from thousands of people blowing their VUVUZELAS (pronounced voo-voo-ZAY-lahs)—long, plastic horns that sound like a swarm of angry bees! The buzzing was so loud during the soccer matches, even the announcers shouting "GOOOOOOOAAAAL!" couldn't compete. South African soccer fans in the 1990s started playing these horns, which quickly became a way to drown out everything: communication between players, referees, and even announcers. Another score for the fans: The vuvuzela is considered one of the MOST ANNOYING (AND INTENSE) SOUNDS in the world!

Choice Nugget

FIFA banned vuvuzelas during the 2014 World Cup. Want to listen for yourself? Check out www.vuvuzela .fm for nonstop vuvuzela noise!

If you CHOSE THAT:

Are you ready to rumble? Just kidding, this song was created to put you to sleep! Three musicians, known as the MARCONI UNION, composed what is thought to be the most relaxing melody ever. The TRIO from Manchester, England, worked with scientists who study the therapeutic aspects of sound to produce this dreamy dirge. So put on your comfy PJs and get ready for some quiet time. The tune's repetition of tones, frequencies, and rhythms encourages a state of super calmness. A study even found that listening to this song is more relaxing than getting a massage. No wonder it's called "Weightless." The song lasts for eight minutes of total CHILL TIME.

CHOOSE **THIS:**

School chorus.

or

CHOOSE **THAT:**

School band.

MUSE BEFORE YOU CHOOSE   Hitting the high notes. Jam sessions. Glee club. Band night.

If you CHOSE ⬇THIS:

Turns out that singing in the school **CHORUS** is good for more than just perfecting your pitch. Chorus members' hearts beat as one—and not just when they're crooning out love songs. When singers **HARMONIZE**, their heartbeats and breathing sync. New research helps explain why. When choir members sing, their heart rates follow the same rhythm, which is guided by the tempo of the song. Researchers think that when singers exhale, nerve impulses activated in the brain cause the heart to beat slower. That means that the **SOOTHING SOUNDS** of choral groups do a lot more for the singers than just make them sound good—they make them feel good too!

If you CHOSE THAT: ⬇

ROCKING OUT in the school band does a whole lot more than get you ready for your own *School of Rock* cameo—your grades will probably benefit too. Studies show that learning to play a musical instrument **BENEFITS** both how your brain develops and how it makes connections between brain cells. And a recent study found that IQ test scores and grades shot up when students started playing instruments. Now that's a score for your report card! So go ahead and rock out. After all, you're just giving your **BRAIN A BOOST!**

Choice Nugget

In 2014, an entire marching band ran the London Marathon together in less than seven hours.

CHOOSE

THIS:

Play a vegetable.

Choice Nugget

If playing real fruit isn't your thing, you can play instruments shaped like fruit, such as an apple-shaped ukulele.

or

CHOOSE

THAT:

Play a fruit.

MUSE
BEFORE YOU
CHOOSE

Pulp. A-*peel*-ing tunes. Mmm ... fruit salad.

If you CHOSE ⬇THIS:

Why simply eat your **VEGETABLES** when you can play them? That's what a band from Vienna, Austria, does. They play all their music on instruments made from vegetables. This group of ten musicians is known as the **VEGETABLE ORCHESTRA**, and pretty much no vegetable is left untouched. Banging on gourds? Blowing through carrots? Playing leeks? It's all in a day's work for these guys. The musicians use drills and other tools to shape the instruments, and then they add microphones and pickups to help amplify the sound. But if you want to start your own veggie band, just make sure your parents don't need the produce for dinner. **PROMISE?**

If you CHOSE ⬇THAT:

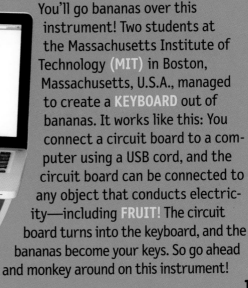

You'll go bananas over this instrument! Two students at the Massachusetts Institute of Technology (**MIT**) in Boston, Massachusetts, U.S.A., managed to create a **KEYBOARD** out of bananas. It works like this: You connect a circuit board to a computer using a USB cord, and the circuit board can be connected to any object that conducts electricity—including **FRUIT!** The circuit board turns into the keyboard, and the bananas become your keys. So go ahead and monkey around on this instrument!

CHOOSE **THIS:**

Ice music.

or

CHOOSE **THAT:**

Volcano
songs.

Frigid notes. Explosive crescendos.

If you CHOSE ↓THIS:

Bundle up in your woolly hat and gloves or this music might just chill you to the bone! In **LAPLAND,** the most northern region in Sweden, a band of intrepid musicians plays music each winter inside a frozen cave. And they play instruments made mostly of ice: *ice*-struments. While the concert hall in Luleå, Sweden, is kept at a cool **23°F** (-5°C), the sound can be sizzling! Just like ice sculptures, the instruments are fragile, and even the slightest warmth from your breath can melt them. The violin, for instance, is hung from the ceiling and played with a protective shield covering its thinner parts, which are just 0.12 inches (3 mm) thick.

If you CHOSE THAT: ↓

Choice Nugget

Mount Etna began to form about half a million years ago.

If fire is more your style, this choice is for you! A scientist uses **MOUNT ETNA,** Europe's tallest active volcano, to create beautiful music. The **10,922-FOOT** (3,330-m)-tall volcano located on the island of Sicily in the Mediterranean Sea has been active since at least 1500 B.C. Giving Etna a voice was the brainchild of Domenico Vicinanza, an Italian scientist who turns patterns in the volcano's movements into sound waves using sonification, a process that translates data into musical notes. And when the song's over, you'll want to erupt into applause!

CHOOSE

THIS:

Rely on your natural talent.

or

CHOOSE

THAT:

Practice makes perfect.

MUSE BEFORE YOU CHOOSE But I'm perfect already? Try and try again. Winging it.

If you CHOSE ↓THIS:

Sometimes people just have natural talent. And new research is proving it. A psychiatrist in London looked at 15,000 IDENTICAL TWINS to see how well they could draw. If one identical twin was good at drawing, then the other twin was more likely to be good at drawing as well. Another study looked at identical Swedish twins who played musical instruments but spent different amounts of time practicing. Guess what? The twin who spent more time PRACTICING didn't necessarily play any better than the slacker twin. So while natural talent does play a role in how good you are at something, don't get too excited. As any Olympic medal winner, concert pianist, or famous artist will tell you, they achieved GREATNESS because they practiced a lot!

If you CHOSE ↓THAT:

Got 10,000 hours to spare? That is 416 days—and the amount of deliberate practice writer MALCOLM GLADWELL and other researchers say it takes to be really awesome at something! By looking at people who excel in their fields, the researchers found that they all had one thing in common—lots and lots of practice. Sure, NATURAL ability has a role, but it's the sweat and toil from hours and hours of practice that really pays off. Pretty cool, huh? So what's the lesson here? You just have to practice. We don't have the saying "PRACTICE MAKES PERFECT" for nothing!

CHOOSE
THIS:

You're
hands-on.

or

CHOOSE
THAT:

You're
hands-off.

If you CHOSE THIS:

MUSE BEFORE YOU CHOOSE

Calloused fingers. Air artistry. Plucking away.

While you might like things hands-on, you might start to think twice after you try to play the **PIKASSO GUITAR**. It has 36 more strings than the standard 6-string version. That's right, this guitar has **42 STRINGS!** The Pikasso also has four necks (well, where else would you put all those strings?) and two sound holes. Surprisingly, it's actually pretty easy to hold because it's thinner where it presses up to your body. The guitar was crafted by hand from Indian rosewood, German spruce, and mahogany. So just like a Pablo Picasso painting, this guitar is a real work of art! But remember, it also took some 1,000 hours of work to build it, so if you ever get your hands on the Pikasso, fret carefully!

If you CHOSE THAT:

Making beautiful music without touching your hands to an instrument sounds like crazy talk. But if you're playing the **THEREMIN**, it'll look just like you are playing the air! The theremin is a musical instrument that uses two metal **ANTENNAS** to control amplitude (how soft or how loud the sound is) and pitch (whether the sound is high or low). The sounds get louder and softer or higher and lower in pitch as you move your hands closer and farther away from the antennas.

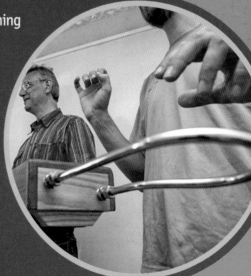

THIS:

Crank it up for all to hear.

or

THAT:

Plug in your headphones.

MUSE BEFORE YOU CHOOSE

Ears ringing. Can't hear the phone ringing. No noise complaints.

If you CHOSE THIS: ⬇

Heads up, Mom and Dad! If you plan to tag along to the next One Direction concert, it's going to get *LOUD!* Sure, we all know the boy band can rock, but add the squeals and cheers of the fans in the audience to the band's sound, and you have noise that goes to a whole new level. One science-minded concertgoer measured the sound, and the FANS didn't disappoint. The squeals and cheers were measured at 122 DECIBELS. That's louder than a screaming arena of hockey fans after a goal, a jet taking off, or the loud boom of a thunderclap!

If you CHOSE ⬇THAT:

Want to hold a dance party at your house but worried about cranky neighbors? If you hold a "SILENT" dance party, the only sound your neighbors will hear is the quiet shuffling of feet! That's because at these parties—around since the 2000s—everyone listens to the same music on his or her own set of headphones. WIRELESS receivers connect the listeners to the music, so there's no need for a booming speaker system. So go ahead and send out the invites. Nobody is going tell you to keep it down!

Choice Nugget

In 2013, the rock band Hedley played a "quiet concert" in Banff National Park in Alberta, Canada, for 1,000 lucky fans.

ANALYZE THIS!

If you mostly picked **CHOOSE THIS,** you thrive on your social life. You live in the moment, enjoying the energy and thrill that comes with being part of a team or in a big crowd. Practicing and improving your skills alone in a room is not your thing. You understand that true inspiration is born through powerful group experiences. Are you sometimes loud and attention-seeking? Perhaps. Are you memorable and awesome? Always.

ANALYZE THAT!

If you mostly picked **CHOOSE THAT,** you're a systematic thinker who uses both the creative and logical sides of your brain. You're one part scientist and one part artist. There is a good chance that one day you'll create the next iPhone on your day job while playing in your band on the weekends. Better yet, you'll go on tour with your famous band and create a popular new app in your free time! I believe your future is limitless when you're a well-rounded thinker with multiple skill sets. That's probably not a shock to hear from me, the psychologist who's also a comedian!

CHAPTER 7

MOBILE MADNESS

Get ready to get moving! From skateboards to roller coasters, this chapter puts a new spin on some old ways to move around and offers some futuristic surprises too. But a quick heads-up—some of these rides are way out there!

CHOOSE
THIS:
Jump aboard a **red wagon** with **74 friends.**

or

CHOOSE
THAT:

Ride a **skateboard** with **20** friends.

MUSE BEFORE YOU CHOOSE Schoolyard charm. Skateboard chic. No time to think twice.

If you CHOSE ⬇THIS:

With its gigantic wheels towering eight feet (2.4 m) above the ground, this ride is definitely not your typical little red wagon. It's ginormous! RADIO FLYER, a company that manufactures traditional wagons and trikes, built this monster to celebrate being in business for 80 YEARS. And while it might look like your childhood ride, the wagon is nine times larger than the one you played with as a kid. Plus it weighs more than the largest AFRICAN ELEPHANT and can easily hold 75 kids. Talk about going big!

If you CHOSE THAT: ⬇

This SKATEBOARD is definitely not one you will want to take with you to school. It's the size of a school bus! This supersize board is just like the ones at the skate park, except, at 36 FEET 7 INCHES (11.2 m) long, it's much, much, much bigger. With such massive length and weight, there's really no way you can airwalk or KICKFLIP with this monstrosity. Twenty people can easily hang out so you and your friends will just have to keep the party rolling!

CHOOSE THIS:

A walk in the park is your speed.

CHOOSE THAT:

Thrills and chills are the way you roll.

MUSE BEFORE YOU CHOOSE

Low-key workout. Losing your lunch. Finished in lightning speed.

If you CHOSE THIS:

If the thought of riding a roller coaster makes you want to hurl, then go ahead and take your chances on the **TIGER & TURTLE** roller coaster in Duisburg, Germany. This steel theme park attraction replaces heart-stopping, high-adrenaline thrills with **249** pedestrian-friendly steps. While it looks like your standard amusement park stomach turner, there's no need to get your nerve up to ride this one! You can walk the ride at your own pace.

If you CHOSE THAT:

Hold on tight, you're heading to the land down under to ride the **TOWER OF TERROR II**—a steel roller coaster in the Dreamworld theme park on Australia's Gold Coast. But you better pack your nerves, because this ride is definitely not for the faint of heart. Since you start off facing a black void, the coaster doesn't reveal all of its heart-stopping, adrenaline-pounding terror right away. No, that happens when you rocket backward at **100 MILES AN HOUR** (161 km/h) in mere seconds. But that's not the end! You then ascend 328 feet (100 m) before hanging weightless, waiting for the ride's next move, which is to drop you in a vertical free fall. Don't worry though, 16,000 bolts keep the ride in place for 40 seconds of screaming fun!

Choice Nugget

A 36-foot (11-m) metallic skull with crimson eyes confronts riders as they enter the Tower of Terror II.

CHOOSE THIS:

Zip across the United States in **less than an hour.**

or

CHOOSE THAT:

Take an **elevator** to the **moon.**

MUSE BEFORE YOU CHOOSE

Never late for a cross-country family birthday. No need to move about the aisles. Lunar levity.

If you CHOSE ↓THIS:

Choice Nugget

The mastermind behind the Hyperloop is the same guy behind SpaceX (see page 51).

Imagine if you could sit back, stretch out, and get from New York City to Los Angeles in less than an hour. Sounds crazy? Well, the HYPERLOOP plans to do just that, and all without having to get on an airplane and mess with stale air and a crowded cabin. The Hyperloop is really just a long vacuum tube that will shoot capsules at speeds approaching 4,000 MILES AN HOUR (6,437 km/h). "Hyper" is right! The idea is to cut down on friction by using magnets to levitate the capsules on a cushion of air. Pretty futuristic, huh? Not exactly—the idea was first presented in an academic paper in 1909.

If you CHOSE THAT: ↓

Have you always wanted to collect a few MOON rocks for yourself? Some day that might be just an elevator ride away. A company based in Seattle, Washington, U.S.A., is working on plans to build an elevator that can carry rocks—and people—to the surface of the moon. The plans call for an electric lifter that will look just like a regular elevator but will slide along a super-strong KEVLAR "ribbon" that connects a station on Earth to a station on the moon. But don't start dreaming about skipping school for a lunar lunch just yet; the team is just testing the feasibility of the plan—a working elevator is decades in the future. Talk about reaching for the moon!

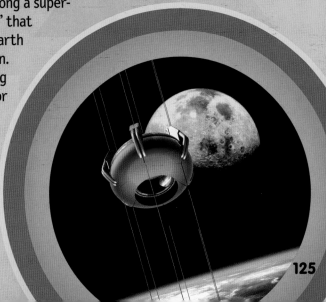

CHOOSE **THIS:**

Keep your shoes **squeaky-clean.**

or

CHOOSE **THAT:**

Get your **feet wet.**

MUSE
BEFORE YOU
CHOOSE

Muddy footprints. Fishy friends. Waterlogged shorts.

If you CHOSE ↓THIS:

Take a jog through the mud and keep your shoes squeaky-clean with the two-wheeled treadmill bike by **BICYCLE FOREST.** The "bike" is really a treadmill on wheels, and it lets you get a workout without your feet ever touching the ground! The treadmill, just like the kind you find in the gym, sits on all-terrain tires that move when you run so they take all the dirt, grime, and punishment—not your shoes. But don't think you've lost all sense of adventure. If you want to get off the city streets and see some greenery, just take this sturdy **TREADMILL** off-road.

If you CHOSE THAT: ↓

Work out in the water and keep your hair dry with the **HYDROWORX** underwater treadmill. This treadmill is at the bottom of a pool so that you can run underwater while keeping your head above the surface to chat with friends. Now that's a win-win! Elite marathon runners use the aquatic workout in their training because the resistance of the water adds an extra challenge. Plus, there's no need to worry about red eyes from **CHLORINE.** So what's the drawback? Well, there's not much of one: You do have to keep track of the time yourself, because electricity to run a clock display and water don't mix. What are you waiting for?

Choice Nugget

Working out in water minimizes the stress on your joints.

127

CHOOSE

THIS:

Never **lace** your **shoes** again.

or

CHOOSE

THAT:

Never **buy** **shoes** again.

MUSE BEFORE YOU CHOOSE

No tripping. Waiting in lines will seem passé. Friends may be envious.

128

If you CHOSE THIS:⬇

If you're the type of person who is always looking for ways to save time, **NIKE MAGS** are the shoes for you. They lace themselves! A designer created these real-life shoes based on the ones worn by Marty McFly, played by Michael J. Fox, in the 1989 hit film *Back to the Future Part II*. In the movie, Marty travels to the future—to 2015 to be exact!—in a time-hopping car and discovers that shoes have really come a long way. But Nike MAGs don't need space-age technology: **MOTORIZED ROLLERS** in the soles sense when someone has stepped into them, and then they tighten the laces automatically. That means instead of spending time fiddling with your laces, you can get to the action fast!

If you CHOSE ⬇THAT:

Are your shoes just not working with your outfit? No problem. You can use a **3-D PRINTER** to bust out a new pair from the comfort of your own room! To create your own unique pair of kicks, all you need is a 3-D printer, a software program, and some thermoplastic polyurethane (that's just a fancy word for a rubberlike material). But while the technology is supercool, it's not superfast. It can take about **TEN HOURS** to print one shoe. You can be patient, right? After all, these shoes are one of a kind!

CHOOSE THIS:

Captain your own submarine.

or

Choice Nugget

Undersea archaeologists used remotely operated vehicles to explore the *Titanic* shipwreck.

CHOOSE THAT:

Pilot your own aircraft.

MUSE BEFORE YOU CHOOSE Giant squid. Shark encounter. Eyes in the sky.

If you CHOSE ⬇THIS:

This **SUB** lets you get up close and personal with sea life whenever and wherever you want. The **TRITON 3300/3** personal submarine has enough room for you and two friends, so you don't have to go it alone. Just climb in through the easy-to-access hatch and set off on your own undersea adventure. Hang out with deep-sea creatures that make their own light at depths of **3,300 FEET** (1,000 m), or roam around a coral reef to find your own Nemo or watch sea turtles. You never know what you might see! After all, it was a Triton sub that first encountered a giant squid living in its underwater environment. You just might want to start saving your pennies now. This submarine costs a cool $3 million!

If you CHOSE ⬇THAT:

The pilot of this **AIRCRAFT** never has to leave the ground. That's because this plane is a drone, a type of aircraft that pilots fly **REMOTELY**. The special drones used by the Air Shepherd Initiative do more that just speed through the clouds. They keep watch over threatened wildlife in southern Africa by sending live video streams to spotters who can look for illegal activity. That's really important, because poaching is a huge problem in the region. Some 40,000 elephants and 1,200 rhinos are killed every year; these are dangerously high numbers considering that fewer than 20,000 rhinos remain in the wild. Computer programs help figure out where the poachers might strike next so that the pilots can fly the drones over at-risk areas. And when poachers are spotted, park rangers waiting on the ground rush to the scene to **PROTECT THE ANIMALS.**

CHOOSE THIS:

Stay dry.

or

CHOOSE THAT:

Perfect hair. No more umbrellas. Water sports.

Get wet.

If you CHOSE THIS:

The rain will never keep you from riding your bike again! The **LEAFX-PRO** is a light plastic shell that attaches to your bike to keep the water out and you raindrop free. The LeafxPro can withstand winds up to **50 MILES** an hour (80 km/h) and still keep you comfortably dry. It's just like a big umbrella for your bike, but one that won't turn inside out in a blast of wind! Since the shell only weighs about three pounds (1.4 kg), you can just fold the contraption up when the sun comes out, and pack it away in a tote that fits on your back.

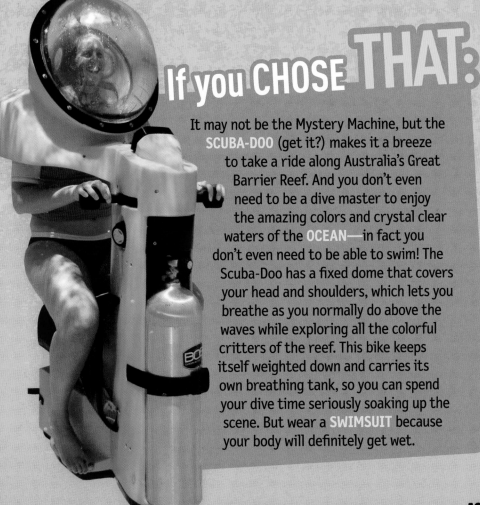

If you CHOSE THAT:

It may not be the Mystery Machine, but the **SCUBA-DOO** (get it?) makes it a breeze to take a ride along Australia's Great Barrier Reef. And you don't even need to be a dive master to enjoy the amazing colors and crystal clear waters of the **OCEAN**—in fact you don't even need to be able to swim! The Scuba-Doo has a fixed dome that covers your head and shoulders, which lets you breathe as you normally do above the waves while exploring all the colorful critters of the reef. This bike keeps itself weighted down and carries its own breathing tank, so you can spend your dive time seriously soaking up the scene. But wear a **SWIMSUIT** because your body will definitely get wet.

LET'S SEE WHAT **YOUR CHOICES** SAY **ABOUT YOU.**

DOC TALK ...

PSYCHOLOGIST DR. MATT BELLACE DISSECTS YOUR DECISIONS ...

ANALYZE
THIS!

If you mostly picked **CHOOSE THIS,** you're an active person who values doing things for yourself. It's not to say that you won't accept help, but you do so only to keep moving on to your next destination. Psychologists refer to people like you as self-actualized. It's a big word that basically means you're a confident person who believes your actions make a difference in the world. It's also unlikely you'll ever get depressed because you're so busy reaching your goals and having fun. That's a nice bonus!

ANALYZE
THAT!

If you mostly picked **CHOOSE THAT,** you'd like people to think you love to exercise, but you actually prefer sweating a little less when getting around. For example, I'm sure you'd like to visit the Egyptian pyramids, as long as an air-conditioned taxi can get you up close. The good part of being less active is you're far less likely to strain a muscle or sweat through your nice shirt. The downside is you miss so many things in life when you stop yourself from just jumping in. Try taking a ride on your bike to somewhere new and see all the things you didn't even know were there!

135

CHAPTER 8

GET FESTIVE

It's all fun and games until someone slips on watermelon guts. Wacky festivals and weird competitions are what this chapter is all about. Want to climb to the top of a tower? Beware! It may be a little wobbly! Have you ever been in a pillow fight that required a bath at the end? When things get festive, sometimes they get a little crazy!

CHOOSE THIS:

Climb onto a **friend's** shoulders.

or

CHOOSE THAT:

Wrestle with a **friend.**

MUSE
BEFORE YOU
CHOOSE

Leaning tower. Stinky feet.

If you CHOSE ↓ THIS:

Don't look down! In the CATALONIA region of Spain, festival activities include one in which as many as 600 people unite to build a human tower, called a *castell*. The tradition began in the beginning of the 19TH CENTURY and developed out of a folk dance. A large base of people—usually the strongest and biggest of the group—forms the base of the TOWER. As individuals climb onto the shoulders of others, the tower grows to as high as nine or ten tiers, with fewer people on each tier as they get higher. The human tower can be as tall as a three-story building! Often nimble and light kids make up the very top tier and raise their hands in the air! Judges don't make their award decisions solely on height, they also base their decisions on the complexity of the build.

Think Twice!

Castells routinely collapse mid-construction, and occasionally there are injuries. For that reason, kids often wear helmets to keep safe in case of a fall.

If you CHOSE THAT: ↓

Put your best foot—er, rather, your *big toe*—forward. In the WORLD TOE WRESTLING CHAMPIONSHIPS in England, opponents lock toes—not unlike locking hands in an arm wrestling competition—and try to overpower one another. In this sport that has been around for 40 years, contestants sit opposite each other and put their feet in a "toedium," where they lock big toes. The object isn't to pin the other person's toe, but rather to push the other players foot out of the bounds. The player to do this the most times out of three rounds is the WINNER.

CHOOSE

THIS:

Play with **ice.**

or

CHOOSE

THAT:

Play with **sand.**

Choice Nugget

The world's tallest sand castle, forged on the beaches of Rio de Janeiro, Brazil, stood 41.25 feet (12.57 m) tall! This was no bucket-and-shovel operation: It was made using five professional earthmoving tractors, and then sculptors came in to do the detail work.

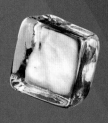

MUSE BEFORE YOU CHOOSE Mittens and earmuffs. Sand buckets and swimsuit.

If you CHOSE ⬇THIS:

Frozen castles, ice slides and mazes, a giant ice sculpture of Cupid ... sounds like the work of *Frozen*'s Elsa! Close—it's the Harbin International Ice and Snow Sculpture Festival in **CHINA**. Hundreds of thousands of people visit the festival every year to tour the **ICE SCULPTURES**—some of which are inspired by Chinese fairy tales and monuments such as the Great Wall—and ice-carved buildings, many of which look distinctly Russian. (Located in northeast China, Harbin isn't far from the Russian border.) Once night falls, the sculptures are illuminated from the inside with colorful lights. While certainly a winter wonderland, don't forget to bundle up—temperatures can get as low as minus 30°F (-34°C)! That's nothing to sneeze at!

If you CHOSE ⬇THAT:

Sand castle *schmand* castle. How about a sand-sculpted woolly mammoth with a little tuft of seaweed on its head? That's the kind of sand art you'll find at the **ANNUAL SCULPTURE CONTEST** at Point Reyes National Seashore in California, U.S.A. Individuals and groups—including kids—face off to create whatever suits their fancies—from Medusa to an Aztec ruin to a sculpture of a man before he's had his morning cup of coffee. Of course, all good things must end. It's not unusual for the sand creations to get **STOMPED** on after prizes have been awarded.

CHOOSE THIS:

Roadkill.

or

CHOOSE THAT:

Mystery meat.

MUSE BEFORE YOU CHOOSE Tastes like chicken. This one is in the can.

If you CHOSE ⬇ THIS:

Have a hankering for some opossum? Maybe a smidgen of squirrel? These are ingredients you can find at the annual **ROADKILL COOK-OFF** in Marlinton, West Virginia, U.S.A. The idea of this festival is not to eat "gross" food, but rather to sample delicious foods that use unconventional meats as an ingredient—from wild boar to porcupine to, yes, **OPOSSUM**.

If you CHOSE THAT:⬇

When you think of Hawaiian cuisine, pineapple, ahi, and even shave ice may come to mind. But don't forget Spam! **SPAM** is a type of canned meat made with pork shoulder, ham, and spices. Why is Spam so popular

in Hawaii? It all started during World War II, when it was served up to soldiers living in **HAWAII**. By the end of the war, Spam had become popular with local islanders, and it continues to be served up for breakfast, lunch, and dinner in homes and restaurants. At the annual Waikiki Spam Jam, you can buy Spam cheesecake, Spam nachos, and even a Spam ice-cream sandwich!

THIS:

Chase a wheel of cheese.

or

THAT:

Ski on watermelon.

Think Twice!

The slope may not be a double black diamond, but even experienced melon skiers have a hard time staying upright. Best protect your melon—meaning your head! Racers wear helmets that are designed to look like watermelons. Safe and stylish!

MUSE BEFORE YOU CHOOSE Roll with it. Melon madness.

144

If you CHOSE ⬇THIS:

What's round, weighs eight pounds (3.5 kg), and rolls down a grassy hill while being chased by frantic runners? A wheel of CHEESE in the traditional cheese-rolling race on Cooper's Hill in Gloucestershire, England, of course! Here's how this wacky race works: The wheel of cheese is released at the top of a hill, and then runners fling themselves after it, sometimes tumbling head over heels down the slope. The first person to make it to the bottom of the hill wins a wheel of cheese! Believe it or not, chasing cheese down hillsides has been an ENGLISH TRADITION since the 19th century.

If you CHOSE ⬇THAT:

When it's summertime in AUSTRALIA, it's time to hit the slopes! Just make sure you bring a change of clothes—not because you'll be wet from making snow angels, but rather you'll be sticky from being covered in WATERMELON juice! At the Chinchilla Melon Festival, a gentle slope is covered in a long strip of black tarp and watermelon guts are smeared all over it. Competitors slip on a pair of watermelon skis (yep, that's right: hollowed-out watermelons you wear on your feet) for a jaunt down the hill. Skiers hold on to a rope that is pulled by runners who race down the length of the tarp. The goal is to stay upright for the entire ride.

CHOOSE THIS:

Savory.

MUSE BEFORE YOU CHOOSE

Garlic breath. Sticky fingers.

CHOOSE THAT:

Sweet.

If you CHOSE THIS:

Bust out the **BREATH MINTS!** The main ingredient for fun at the Gilroy Garlic Festival is garlic! Held every summer in the town of Gilroy, in central California, U.S.A., the festival is for foodies who love all things garlic. (You definitely won't find any vampires in this town.) On the menu for tasting: garlic crawdads, garlic noodles, and even garlic ice cream. Gilroy has been dubbed the **"GARLIC CAPITAL OF THE WORLD,"** as most of the world's minced, pickled, and powdered garlic is processed there. Besides enjoying the food and a cook-off, you can even buy yourself a hat that looks like a head of garlic!

If you CHOSE THAT:

You can whoop it up at the **WHOOPIE PIE** Festival in Pennsylvania Dutch Country, U.S.A. At this annual festival, kids can go on a **TREASURE HUNT** to find hidden whoopie pies, play a game of checkers using whoopie pies as game pieces, or give a holler at the "whoopie yell off," where the loudest "Whoopie!" wins. But whoopie pies aren't just for play—you can eat them too! Of course there is a whoopie pie-eating contest, where competitors clock how many pies they can eat in a given time, but you can also sit back, relax, and try more than 100 different flavors of the gooey treat.

THIS:

Play chess.

or

CHOOSE

THAT:

Have a
pillow fight.

MUSE BEFORE YOU CHOOSE Use your noggin. Flying feathers.

If you CHOSE THIS: ⬇

CHESSBOXING requires the fitness and power of a boxer and the brains and focus of a chess player. The competition that brings together this unlikely pairing has been around for more than 30 years. Here's how it works: Players are matched just like in a boxing match—similar weights, abilities, and experience. Opponents play a round of chess—on a table in the middle of a BOXING RING—that lasts about four minutes. They wear headphones with blaring music to keep out the noise from the announcer, who entertains the crowd with a play-by-play of the chess match. When the bell rings, the table is moved, and it's time to box! This goes on for 11 rounds or until someone gets checkmated or someone is knocked out!

If you CHOSE ⬇THAT:

The World Pillow Fighting Championships, held in Northern California, U.S.A., are not your average sleepover pillow fights. They're serious! Two people, each wielding a PILLOW, of course, straddle a large metal pole that spans a mud pit. During the pillow fight, they can't hold onto the pole with their hands at all for support. To make matters more difficult, they can only block their opponent's swinging pillow—they can't grab it. A referee keeps an eye out for foul play, and no resting is allowed. HERE'S THE BAD NEWS: You lose by falling off the pole and landing in the muddy pond below!

Choice Nugget

April 4 has been proclaimed International Pillow Fight Day, when people around the world, with pillows in hand, gather in public spaces to have it out with strangers. Generally, the rules are simple: A whistle is blown, people whack each other for a given period of time—sometimes as long as two hours—another whistle is blown, and feathers are picked up!

CHOOSE THIS:

Embrace the night.

or

CHOOSE THAT:

Celebrate the sun.

MUSE
BEFORE YOU
CHOOSE

Careful carving.
Dancing in
the street.

If you CHOSE THIS:

In Oaxaca, Mexico, Christmastime—not Halloween—is the season for **CARVING VEGETABLES.** Noche de Rábanos (Night of the Radishes) is a century-old tradition in which locals **CARVE** radishes for an annual nighttime competition held two days before Christmas. In Oaxaca's main plaza, farmers and artisans show off their radish sculptures, of which Maya rulers, Christian religious figures, and local wildlife are often the subjects. Fans of the **RADISH ART** wait in long lines to pass by the artists' booths to get glimpses of their work. But alas, these sculptures are temporary: They turn brown and have to be tossed after only a few days.

If you CHOSE THAT:

Traditionally, during the time of the Inca Empire, Inti Raymi (Festival of the Sun) was a **NINE-DAY CELEBRATION** to honor the sun god during winter solstice (when the sun is the farthest from Earth). Today, a festival in Cusco, Peru, honors that **500-YEAR-OLD TRADITION.** An actor portraying an Inca emperor rides in a chariot through city streets, which are filled with music and people dancing. Historically an animal was ceremonially **SACRIFICED** to ensure good crops, but today that sacrifice is faked. Hundreds of thousands of tourists and locals come to the city every year to watch the ceremony, eat food, and dance.

ANALYZE
THIS!

If you mostly picked **CHOOSE THIS,** your idea of a vacation involves being really hands-on and engaged in an activity. Your personality style means that you do not enjoy sitting around and watching the flowers grow. You'd prefer to plant a garden or two while others look on. If you're stuck inside, you'd rather dominate in Monopoly than just watch some television. You may be described as the "life of the party," since you're so willing to get involved. The only downside is you might need a vacation from your vacation to rest up!

ANALYZE
THAT!

If you mostly picked **CHOOSE THAT,** you're a fun-loving person who enjoys a good laugh. You don't take yourself too seriously and understand the value of stepping out of your comfort zone. Your personality style is upbeat and very likable. If you were a puppy or a bunny, everyone would want to pet your head. In fact, you would make a natural comedian because you're so likable. Your smile is contagious. You draw people in with your easy-going ways and love for life.

CHAPTER **9**

PICK YOUR BRAIN

How well do you know yourself? Pretty well, eh? Are you sure? Your answers in this chapter might surprise you! This last chapter is all about figuring out what makes you tick. Are you a lone wolf type or do you like to hang with the crowd? Are you fierce and in charge or graceful and whimsical? Turn the page and fire up those neurons to make some decisions.

CHOOSE THIS:

Stay home.

CHOOSE THAT:

Wander.

MUSE BEFORE YOU CHOOSE

Home is where the heart is. The world is your oyster. Cabin fever. Tired feet.

Choice Nugget

In Greek mythology, Hermes shepherded the dead to Hades, also known as the underworld.

If you CHOSE THIS:

Turns out that if you like hanging around the house, you have a lot in common with the Greek goddess **HESTIA.** She was the goddess of the hearth, which means Hestia was the ultimate homebody! She was also super kind and forgiving, so much so that both the god of the sea (Poseidon) and the god of sun and music (Apollo) wanted to marry her. Hestia turned them both down. In ancient **GREECE,** when a new colony was established, a flame from her hearth would be carried to the new town to start the hearth there, which was supposed to bring luck. Does this remind you of something? It should! In ancient Greece, fire was considered to be a divine element representing purity. That symbolism carries over today in the lighting of the Olympic torch.

If you CHOSE THAT:

If you're one to rarely put your feet up, you have a lot in common with **HERMES,** the Greek messenger of the gods. Hermes was always on the go, and for important reasons. When he delivered a message, the other gods paid attention! Imagine cruising around in winged golden sandals to deliver messages in a **FLASH.**

CHOOSE **THIS:**

You are a
picky eater.

or

CHOOSE **THAT:**

You **clean**
your **plate.**

MUSE BEFORE YOU CHOOSE

You're not picky—you just have standards! Food coma.

If you CHOSE ⬇THIS:

Sometimes it's nice to keep things predictable—like having the exact same thing for dinner every night. If you're a **KOALA**, that same menu extends to breakfast and lunch! These furry Australian marsupials always know what's going to be on their menu—eucalyptus leaves. Not only that, koalas are even **PICKY** when it comes to what kind of eucalyptus leaves they'll chew. Out of some 900 different species of eucalyptus, koalas like to eat only about 40 to 50 different varieties. And within those types, they only really like 10. Talk about a picky eater!

If you CHOSE THAT:⬇

Chomp chomp! If you devour your dinner like there's no tomorrow, you can put yourself in the same camp as the spotted hyena. This African **CARNIVORE** can really polish off a meal! Once a **HYENA** starts to chow down, nothing stands in its way. Bones, hooves, and even teeth pose no problem for the hyena's strong jaws. And when these carnivores (animals that eat meat) snag a meal, they make a noise that sounds a lot like a human giggle. But the hyenas aren't laughing at their dinner—the sound alerts others in their pack that food is around. Since packs can contain as many as 80 other hyenas, that's a whole lot of munching.

CHOOSE THIS:
Comic books.

or

CHOOSE THAT:
Rare coins.

MUSE BEFORE YOU CHOOSE Lazy afternoons reading on the sofa. Change jingling in your pocket.

If you CHOSE ↓THIS:

All that COMIC BOOK collecting might one day pay off (and in more ways than just an entertaining afternoon spent fighting villains). In 1938 you could buy a copy of *Action Comics* No. 1, which featured SUPERMAN lifting a car on the cover, for just ten cents! Today, that same book would cost you $2.16 million! At least, that's what one collector paid for an issue in late 2011. This particular comic was stolen in 2000 but later recovered in a storage locker. Talk about a lucky find!

If you CHOSE ↓THAT:

Bet you didn't know that a PENNY could be worth MILLIONS? That's exactly what happened in early 2015 with a penny from 1793 known as the "chain cent." It sold for $2.35 million! Why so pricey? The design of the penny was changed quickly after it was first produced, so this particular coin is incredibly RARE. And why is it called a chain cent? The back of this penny has a chain with 15 linking rings, representing the 15 states at the time. That design was soon changed from rings to a wreath. So the next time you see a penny on the ground, pick it up! Who knows, it might be worth more than just GOOD LUCK.

CHOOSE THIS:

You surround yourself with **friends.**

or

CHOOSE THAT:

You'd rather go **solo.**

MUSE BEFORE YOU CHOOSE Leader of the pack. Alone time. Crowds. Lone wolf.

If you CHOSE ↓THIS:

Traveling in a **PACK** is where it's at for Atlantic herring. In fact, you'll never find them swimming solo! These silvery **FISH** live in the northern Atlantic Ocean and like to stick together and travel in humongous schools of hundreds of thousands of fish. If you happened to be swimming underneath such a gigantic school, it would block out the sun! What's the point of moving in such a large crowd? Well, that's the point exactly—being surrounded by so many other fish helps keep most of the school safe from hungry seals and whales. Now that's safety in numbers!

If you CHOSE ↓THAT:

WOLVERINES don't bother hanging out with the group. Instead they go it alone. But they do like to hit the road! The solitary life of these forest mammals means that wolverines can travel some **15 MILES** (24 km) in just one day to search for food, which can be tough in the northern forests of Siberia and North America that they call home. These tough predators will grab some berries and plants, but what they really love to feast on is meat. Wolverines will even wake up hibernating mammals just to chomp into them. How rude!

Think Twice!

Wolverines are also called carcajous, Indian devils, or skunk bears.

CHOOSE

THIS:

Lion.

or

CHOOSE

THAT:

Dragonfly.

Think Twice!

Young lions usually start hunting when they are about one year old.

MUSE BEFORE YOU CHOOSE

Fierceness. Flight. Magnificent mane. Whimsical wings.

If you CHOSE ⬇THIS:

The KING of the beasts for you, right? While the intimidating size of African lions strikes fear in the hearts of creatures on the savanna, those animals really shouldn't spend all their time worrying about an attack. Why not? LIONS catch only about a quarter of all the animals they chase. Those odds mean that three out of four zebras make it out of the chase alive. While hunting strategies differ between lion kings and queens (lionesses cooperate while hunting, while male lions like to ambush their dinner from a hiding spot in dense grass), these mighty hunters might not be so terrifying after all!

If you CHOSE THAT:⬇

Delicate, flitting, and floating past. Not so fast! DRAGONFLIES may be dainty and beautiful to watch, but these brutally efficient hunters kill about 95 percent of the insects they attack—and they do it in midair. That means that if a dragonfly is eyeing you for dinner, your time is probably up. These voracious fliers snag their prey, then mash and munch it—often while FLYING! A dragonfly's four wings can maneuver independently, helping it reach speeds of up to 30 miles an hour (48 km/h).

CHOOSE THIS:

Face the future.

or

CHOOSE THAT:

Pick the past.

If you CHOSE THIS:

Settling into an airline seat made from plants might sound a little strange, but for the inventors at Airbus, it may just be the wave of the future. **ENGINEERS** at the airplane manufacturer are looking to nature to figure out ways to make air travel more environmentally friendly, and that includes using plant-based fabrics that can grow into specialized shapes for seats. These airline architects are asking many questions to help determine the future of air travel. It's a good thing these designers have their heads in the clouds!

If you CHOSE THAT:

Choice Nugget

To pass time on these long sea voyages, Vikings played board games and recited stories.

A National Geographic Expeditions cruise lets you travel back in time to follow the path of the famous tenth-century explorers—the **VIKINGS.** Just imagine: You might lean over the ship's railing and come face-to-face with Norse explorer Erik the Red! But your journey isn't going to be as tough as it was for those **ANCIENT** seafarers. Instead of being tossed around on a Viking ship, you'll be traveling in comfort on a cruise liner that has a sauna for relaxation and a library where you can brush up on all things Scandinavian.

CHOOSE

THIS:

Private gallery.

or

CHOOSE

THAT:

Public art.

Think Twice!

Doodling can help keep your brain focused. Drawing holds your attention just enough that when you start to get bored, you don't drift off to the land of daydreams.

MUSE BEFORE YOU CHOOSE

Pen and ink. Spray cans and stepladders. Security details.

If you CHOSE ⬇THIS:

Do you ever **DOODLE** in class when your mind starts to wander? Well, you're not alone. In fact, many famous people throughout **HISTORY** have been doodlers, including American presidents! President George Washington doodled geometric shapes. President Thomas Jefferson drew a machine to make macaroni (yep, you read that right). President Andrew Jackson doodled an alligator. But it doesn't stop there. President Barack Obama doodles too—often the faces of people in his meetings!

If you CHOSE THAT:⬇

Like to show off your artistic creations for the whole world to see? You'll feel right at home in São Paulo, Brazil. Some **21 MILLION PEOPLE** live in this South American city and its surrounding areas, and its vivid street art is impossible to overlook. While outdoor advertising has been banned in the city since 2006, street art has helped fill the void, giving the city a colorful, creative vibe. Want to see some local art? Head over to **BATMAN'S ALLEY,** where the walls are canvases for funky designs. Or take a gander at a project known as Projeto 4km—a strip where 70 urban artists took their creativity to a 2.5-mile (4-km) stretch of buildings along the way to a soccer stadium that hosted matches during the 2014 FIFA World Cup.

169

CHOOSE **THIS:**

Find your inner balance.

or

CHOOSE **THAT:**

Use your physical strength.

Choice Nugget

According to the U.S. Coast Guard, paddleboards are considered vessels. Ahoy, matey!

MUSE BEFORE YOU CHOOSE

Stretching in a Zen state. Muscle burn. No pain, no gain.

If you CHOSE ⬇THIS:

The gentle exercises of this yoga workout will make you feel like you are floating—on water that is! That's because this yoga routine is done while balancing on a **PADDLEBOARD.** You've probably seen paddleboarders cruising along, rowing with a long oar. In S.U.P. (stand-up paddleboarding) yoga, in addition to paddling, you perform poses while gliding with the waves. Since you have to remain balanced on the board, you have to pay super-close attention to your **FORM.** Otherwise your downward dog might just put you in the water!

If you CHOSE THAT:⬇

Hanging from a sheer granite rock wall calls for a ton of physical strength. And visitors to California's **YOSEMITE NATIONAL PARK** in January 2015 got to see such an incredible feat of strength firsthand. All they had to do was to look up at the vertical rock face known as El Capitan to watch two climbers hang from their fingertips, holding on to only the smallest slivers of rock. The climbers, Tommy Caldwell and Kevin Jorgeson, made history when they became the first to free-climb the entire **3,000-FOOT** (914-m) slab. For 19 days the two only used their fingertips and feet to hang on to the natural curves of the rock. Don't worry: They were attached to safety ropes in case they fell!

ANALYZE
THIS!

If you mostly picked **CHOOSE THIS,** you have a tough exterior, but on the inside you're just a big cupcake. You'd like the world to see you as big and strong, so you like to show your physical strength and surround yourself with the protection of lots of friends. However, when given a choice you'd take a good book or a meal at home over being out with those friends most days of the week. You really don't like confrontation. You hope to scare away threats so that you can just be in your own head and relax.

ANALYZE
THAT!

If you mostly picked **CHOOSE THAT,** your brain (and body) move faster than the rest of the world. In many ways, the brain is like a computer. It has a certain processing speed, and as you know, some people are set to slow! When these people visit your town, they walk around at a glacial pace compared to your natural speedy stride. You're the type of person who is done with a test super early, and you do well! When you go hiking, you lap other people with ease. Your favorite activity involves breaking your own records. The only problem is you often find yourself alone because no one can keep up!

Credits

Matt Bellace illustrations by Joe Rocco.

COVER: (gummy bears), Viktor1/Shutterstock; (chocolates), M. Unal Ozmen/Shutterstock; (airplane), IM_photo/Shutterstock; (cruise ship) NAN728/Shutterstock; Back cover: (UP LE and UP CTR), Justin Tallis/Getty Images; (UP RT), Newspix/Getty Images

FRONT MATTER: 2 (LE), Cinagro/Splash News/Newscom; 2 (RT), Caters News/Newscom; 3 (LE), Martin Harvey/Alamy; 3 (RT), iStock.com/Kelvinyam; **CHAPTER 1:** 8-9, varuna/Shutterstock; 10 (UP), Zade Rosenthal/© Walt Disney Studios Motion Pictures/Courtesy Everett Collection; 10-11 (LO), Cyril Ruoso/Minden Pictures; 11 (UP), iStock.com/Lightboxx; 12-13 (UP), Kim Taylor/Minden Pictures; 13 (LO), © Sony Pictures/Courtesy Everett Collection; 14-15 (UP), Maros Bauer/Shutterstock; 14 (LO), © 20th Century Fox Film Corp. All rights reserved/Courtesy Everett Collection; 14 (LE), © Walt Disney Studios Motion Pictures/Courtesy Everett Collection; 15 (RT), ÊReinhard Dirscherl/SeaPics.com; 16, f9photos/Shutterstock; 17, iStock.com/studio7; 17 (LO), Enrique R Aguirre Aves/Getty Images; 18-19 (UP), Walter Iooss Jr./Getty Images; 19 (LO), Vilainecrevette/Shutterstock; 20, iStock.com/mevans; 20-21 (UP), Matthew Horwood/Getty Images; 21 (LO), iStock.com/Flander; 22, iStock.com/julos; 22-23 (UP), Pete Oxford/Minden Pictures; 22-23 (LO), iStock.com/Jonathan Pledger; 24-25 (LO), Westend61/Getty Images; 25 (UP), iStock.com/EcoPic; 26-27 (LO), Patrick Foto/Shutterstock; 27 (UP), iStock.com/william87; **CHAPTER 2:** 28-29, Peter Dazeley/Getty Images; 30 (UP), iStock.com/frankoppermann; 30 (LO), iStock.com/Necip Yanmaz; 30-31 (LO), iStock.com/Necip Yanmaz; 31 (UP), iStock.com/floridastock; 32 (UP), iStock.com/jamesbenet; 32 (LO), 2xSamara.com/Shutterstock; 33 (UP), iStock.com/elguiri; 33 (LO), iStock.com/efesan; 34-35 (UP), iStock.com/d9tech; 35 (LO), Aurora Photos/Alamy; 36, iStock.com/Aldo Murillo; 36, Piotr Marcinski/Shutterstock; 37, NASA/Alamy; 37 (LO), Henn Photography/Getty Images; 38 (LE), Krasowit/Shutterstock; 38 (RT), JonMilnes/Shutterstock; 39, Natalie Fobes/Getty Images; 39 (LO), Stocktrek Images/Getty Images; 40-41, Aaron Huey/National Geographic Creative/Corbis; 41 (UP), WPA Pool/Getty Images; 41 (RT), James Burke/The LIFE Picture Collection/Getty Images; 42 (UP LE), photka/Shutterstock; 42 (UP RT), Paolo Bona/Shutterstock; 43-43 (LO), PavleMarjanovic/Shutterstock; 44-45 (LO), Annette Shaff/Shutterstock; 45 (UP), Kues/Shutterstock; **CHAPTER 3:** 46-47, Science Photo Library - Victor Habbick Visions/Getty Images; 48-49 (UP), AP Photo/Rex Features; 48 (LO), AP Photo/Rex Features; 49 (UP), Science & Society Picture Library/Getty Images; 49 (LO), NASA/Time Life Picture Collection/Getty Images; 50 (UP), tobkatrina/Shutterstock; 50 (LO), iStock.com/Clicknique; 50-51 (LO CTR), Science & Society Picture Library/Getty Images; 51, Pascal Le Segretain/Getty Images; 52 (UP), iStock.com/SpiffyJ; 52 (LO), NASA; 53 (UP), iStock.com/fredrikarnell; 54 (UP), Hulton Archive/Getty Images; 54-55 (LO), Bryan Sikora/Alamy; 55 (UP), Volt Collection/Shutterstock; 56-57 (CTR), NASA/Getty Images; 57 (UP), Kate Allen/The Toronto Star/ZUMAPRESS.com/Newscom; 57 (LO LE), NASA; 58 (UP), iStock.com/cnrn; 58 (LO LE), NASA/Getty Images; 58-59 (CTR), Bill Ingalls/NASA/Getty Images; 59 (UP), JPL/NASA; 60-61 (UP CTR), Caspar Benson/Getty Images; 60 (UP LE), blackred/Getty Images; 60 (LO), Hero Images/Getty Images; 61 (UP RT), Time Life Pictures/Getty Images; 62, Zurijeta/Shutterstock; 63 (UP), Science & Society Picture Library/Getty Images; **CHAPTER 4:** 64-65, Brand New Images/Getty Images; 66-67 (UP), iStock.com/Noppasin Wongchum; 66 (LO), Michael Courtney/Shutterstock; 67 (LO), Clark James Mishler Photography; 68-69 (UP), Viesti Associates, Inc.; 68-69 (LO), Geoff Swaine/LFI/Newscom; 69 (RT), Geoff Swaine/LFI/Newscom; 70-71 (UP), Cinagro/Splash News/Newscom; 71 (LO), Caters News/ZUMAPRESS.com/Newscom; 72 (UP LE), Solent News/Splash News/Newscom; 72 (LO), iStock.com/sumnersgraphicsinc; 73 (UP LE), Solent News/Splash News/Newscom; 73, WENN.com/Newscom; 74-75 (UP CTR), Roger Tidman/NHPA/Photoshot/Newscom/Newscom; 75, Courtesy Get Shaved Ice; 76, iStock.com/AbbieImages; 77 (UP), iStock.com/AaronAmat; 77 (LO), iStock.com/Spencer Gordon; 78, ThinkGeek/Splash News/Newscom; 78 (LO), Carol Sharp/Flowerphotos/Newscom; 79 (UP), The Colombian Way Ltda/Getty Images; 79 (LO), Colin Underhill/Alamy; 80-81, Science Photo Library/Alamy; 81 (UP), Poznyakov/Shutterstock; **CHAPTER 5:** 82-83, Jordan Siemens/Getty Images; 84 (UP), Mitchell Funk/Getty Images; 84-85 (LO), Babak Tafreshi/Getty Images; 85 (UP RT), Sylvain Sonnet/Getty Images; 86 (UP), Karl Johaentges/Robert Harding World Imagery; 86-87 (LO), Fb-Fischer/Robert Harding World Imagery; 87 (UP), Florian Graner/Minden Pictures; 88 (LE), Michael Marquand/Getty Images; 89 (UP), Brian Cahn/ZUMApress.com/Newscom; 89 (LO), iStock.com/Aneese; 90 (UP),

Staff for This Book
Ariane Szu-Tu, *Project Editor*
Jim Hiscott, *Art Director*
Nicole Lazarus, *Designer*
Hillary Leo, *Photo Editor*
Paige Towler, *Editorial Assistant*
Michaela Weglinski, *Special Projects Assistant*
Sanjida Rashid and Rachel Kenny, *Design Production Assistants*
Tammi Colleary-Loach, *Rights Clearance Manager*
Michael Cassady and Mari Robinson, *Rights Clearance Specialists*
Grace Hill, *Managing Editor*
Joan Gossett, *Senior Production Editor*
Lewis R. Bassford, *Production Manager*
George Bounelis, *Manager, Production Services*
Susan Borke, *Legal and Business Affairs*

Published by the National Geographic Society
Gary E. Knell, *President and CEO*
John M. Fahey, *Chairman of the Board*
Melina Gerosa Bellows, *Chief Education Officer*
Declan Moore, *Chief Media Officer*
Hector Sierra, *Senior Vice President and General Manager,
    Book Division*

Senior Management Team, Kids Publishing and Media
Nancy Laties Feresten, *Senior Vice President;* Erica Green, *Vice President, Editorial Director, Kids Books;* Amanda Larsen, *Design Director, Kids Books;* Jennifer Emmett, *Vice President, Content;* Eva Absher-Schantz, *Vice President, Visual Identity;* Rachel Buchholz, *Editor and Vice President,* NG Kids *magazine;* Jay Sumner, *Photo Director;* Hannah August, *Marketing Director;* R. Gary Colbert, *Production Director*

Digital
Laura Goertzel, *Manager;* Sara Zeglin, *Senior Producer;* Bianca Bowman, *Assistant Producer;* Natalie Jones, *Senior Product Manager*